All about Strips

Colorful Quilts from Strips of Many Sizes

Susan Guzman

Martingale
Create with Confidence

Dedication

For my husband, Ervin. I thank you for the love, encouragement, and time you've given to support my craft. I will always treasure how you've had my creative back from the start. I would not be doing what I love without your confidence in what I do. I love you.

All about Strips:
Colorful Quilts from Strips of Many Sizes
© 2015 by Susan Guzman

Martingale®
19021 120th Ave. NE, Ste. 102
Bothell, WA 98011-9511 USA
ShopMartingale.com

Printed in China
20 19 18 17 16 15   8 7 6 5 4 3 2

Library of Congress Cataloging-in-Publication Data is available upon request.

ISBN: 978-1-60468-474-2

Mission Statement

Dedicated to providing quality products and service to inspire creativity.

Credits

PUBLISHER AND CHIEF VISIONARY OFFICER:
  Jennifer Erbe Keltner

EDITOR IN CHIEF: Mary V. Green

DESIGN DIRECTOR: Paula Schlosser

MANAGING EDITOR: Karen Costello Soltys

ACQUISITIONS EDITOR: Karen M. Burns

TECHNICAL EDITOR: Nancy Mahoney

COPY EDITOR: Sheila Chapman Ryan

PRODUCTION MANAGER: Regina Girard

COVER AND INTERIOR DESIGNER: Connor Chin

PHOTOGRAPHER: Brent Kane

ILLUSTRATOR: Lisa Lauch

Contents

Since I was a young girl, I've admired designs with strong form and color. I find beauty in the details of my environment; whether it's a staircase with an engraved banister or a carved surround to a fireplace, my interest magnifies as I study the artistry of the details. Much of what I know about design is from paying attention to the small touches—and to my instinct. I'm a self-taught quilt designer who has gleaned skills from prior experiences in the creative marketplace.

When working with fabric companies and magazines, a designer must adhere to certain guidelines and design for a particular audience of fans and subscribers. When I'm able to, I insert more of what I personally like, including fabrics with lots of interesting color and pattern. In my designs, I want to show off the fabrics as best I can to enjoy the beauty of the fabrics in big pieces; I prefer not to cut up beautiful prints.

My design style tends to be eclectic. It has a modern appeal with traditional roots, inspired by my love of architectural elements, interior design, and quilts from the past. I like designing clean-line quilts that can be jazzed up with vibrant, exciting color. I also love a neutral palette for a more refined look and appreciate the calming effect of neutral colors.

While deciding what quilt designs to include in this book, I wanted to be sure that the body of work would encompass a collection of timeless, modern quilt designs that anyone can make. I also wanted the designs to be diverse enough so that you could easily show off your favorite stash fabrics or designer collections. In addition, I wanted to keep the writing personal, as if you were spending time with a good friend, and to include tips and suggestions on how to discover new ways of choosing color and looking at inspiring images.

My hope is that through this book, you'll more clearly understand and appreciate *your* unique style; it's such an important part of who you are, the decisions you make, and what you define as appealing.

I'm often overwhelmed by the color wheel. Yes, it's true—and that's coming from someone who has worked with color and design professionally for almost 20 years. I know. Please don't cringe.

As far back as I can remember, I've instinctually known what I like as far as color and style are concerned, and have always felt confident in choosing what I feel works. Call me a rebel, but I would rather select colors from nature, a favorite photograph or magazine image, a colorful piece of cloth, or a beautiful painting from the Italian Renaissance than use the color wheel to select colors for a quilt. Using the color wheel allows for too many opportunities to second-guess myself; I feel less pressure if I rely on my gut to tell me what works, and I trust it.

In the following section are some general principles to help you understand color, including tint, shade, and tone. That way you can feel confident in choosing your own color palette, rather than relying on using a bundle of precut strips.

Colors and Mood

Colors can influence our mood, creating a sense of excitement, serenity, or even melancholy. Some colors can invoke perception, such as when you see a particular color, another one of your senses (taste, or sound, perhaps?) is also stimulated.

Pink. A certain hue of pink can invoke the taste of sweetness, so it's become a favored color for pastries and candy. Feng Shui principles recommend painting the walls of a bedroom pink because it's serene and calming. What a novel idea for those of us with hurried lifestyles, and for those who have trouble sleeping.

Orange. On the contrary, orange is associated with loudness, such as the vibrations you feel when a trumpet is blown.

Red. Advertising agencies take full advantage of subconscious responses from their intended audience. Viewing the color red, for example, releases adrenaline, creating excitement; blood pressure can rise and breathing becomes faster. Crazy, right? It's also known that the color red stimulates one's appetite. There have been claims that food tastes even better in a red environment and, as a former interior designer, I often used a shade of red in a kitchen or dining room.

Yellow. There's a reason caution signs are yellow; yellow is a warning color. To use nature as an example, a variety of insects with bright-yellow markings have poisonous stings or bites, like bees or wasps. Their yellow-and-black combination makes us pull back; we aren't willing to go near for fear of being stung. Babies are more likely to cry in a yellow environment and people, in general, can become anxious and lose their tempers when surrounded by yellow. Yellow is also synonymous with speed and is often used on sports cars.

Blue. So what color brings about feelings of respect, safety, and authority? Blue. Blue is persuasive. It's calming and safe. Think about a cloudless blue sky on a sunny day: doesn't your mood become cool, calm, and collected? Blue gives us the feeling that time is endless.

Green. The color green, too, has a calming effect. It's cool and comforting. Imagine walking in a forest in the middle of summer, with trees at their peak of color. This sense of peace is how I define green.

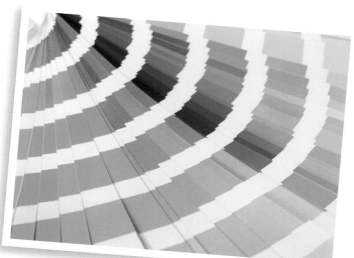

Color Inspiration

What sort of mood do you wish to capture in your quilt? Is it the variety of color from moment to moment during a sunset or the vibrant hues of a public garden? Maybe the rich, earthy, tone-on-tone greens and browns of a forest? Or the open waters of the sea with a variety of blues and greens? Pulling inspiration from your environment will give you endless ideas for color palettes that nature creates for you. Color resources at your fingertips include:

Favorite magazines. I enjoy gleaning inspiration from current fashion and decor magazines. I find loads of ideas simply by looking at a watchband, high-fashion clothing, the design of a perfume bottle, or a decorative fireplace or piece of furniture. My quilts, "Bookshelves" (page 28), "Rogue" (page 35), and "Garden Mews" (page 62) were inspired by magazine images.

Your home. Look at colors pulled from an area rug or oriental carpet, an art print or painting. Our house was being packed by movers when I came up with the design for "Drawers" (page 50) as I saw one of our dressers move past me to be secured in the moving van.

Online images. Search for things you enjoy. For example, I love the paintings of the Italian Renaissance, so searching for this subject online provides a huge amount of color and design inspiration.

Museum or library websites. Or go in person. Take a sketchbook to jot down or sketch out ideas.

Create a design-ideas file. Store images for future reference. This can be an actual paper file, where you can store pages from magazines, or a digital file where you save images from online searches. There are endless ideas that can stem from doing this.

For example, let's say you came across an image in a magazine of a beautifully decorated living room. Look around the room at the variety of visual textures. Take note of the different fabrics used on the furniture and window treatments and ask yourself: How many different fabrics are used? How many colors are used? Keep in mind how a variety of textures and colors can add interest to your quilts—just as they do in room design. Taking snapshots or tearing out pages from magazines of the things that bring you joy and taking them with you to your local quilt shop will help you to learn more about color and pattern. Eventually you'll find that you won't need to bring anything with you and will instinctually know what you're looking for. Practicing these actions will make coordinating fabrics for a quilt second-nature.

Tips for Coloring a Design

Proper placement of color and pattern are key to a successful quilt design. Anchor certain elements to bring cohesiveness to your projects. For example, selecting a common element of color to place across your quilt top will allow places for the viewer's eye to rest, neutralizing and anchoring the entire design.

Neutralize busy fabrics. You can calm busy fabrics by introducing black, white, or other neutrals, as I did with Amy Butler's Hapi collection in "Garden Mews" (page 62). The Hapi collection is bold and vibrant and I wanted to find a way to combine the fabrics without too much visual competition. I added the dark gray and ivory to create "gardens" by corralling the prints with simple, interesting rows of neutral color. The sashing is reminiscent of a walled garden.

Have a common denominator for cohesiveness. Whether it's using the same cream solid for all the drawer pulls in "Drawers" (page 50) or using the same orange print for the vertical background strips in "Flair" (below left and on page 39), these common elements help ground the designs. In "Bookshelves" (page 28), the sashing pieces differ in color, but they use the same striped print. Finally, in "Kindred Spirit" (below and on page 58), the sashing strips have slight variations in color, which adds visual interest, yet the overall design remains cohesive.

Flair

Kindred Spirit

Tips for Coloring Scrappy Quilts

For scrappy quilts, take the following into consideration:

- **The more the merrier!** I love a fun social event and I truly believe the fabrics in our stash can be just as social as we are. Group them together en masse!

- **Always use elements in odd numbers.** I guarantee it will make a much more appealing quilt. There's something about odd numbers that adds to the visual party.

- **Include variety.** All of these elements add loads of interest: various print scale; florals, geometrics, and solids; saturated, medium, and light colors.

- **Start with the attention-getting colors.** Whether using prints or solids, place the reds, fuchsias, oranges or other bold fabrics on your design wall first. With this technique, you're placing the boldest fabrics in key areas of your quilt. It's like real estate: location, location, location.

- **Place same-print fabrics in a zigzag fashion.** Spread them out across the quilt design in a zigzag pattern from top to bottom. I like to start in the top-left corner of my quilt. As I color the quilt, and the uncolored areas begin to fill up, I change my starting point to the upper-right corner of my quilt. "Garden Mews" is a great example to study.

- **Don't be afraid to make changes.** Be aware that when you get down to the last few fabrics, you may want to move a few around so that you don't have two of the same patches right next to each other. However, I always leave my favorites where I originally placed them.

I've found that arranging the fabrics in my quilts in this way allows for a no-fail, attractive quilt. Placing random patches in this manner adds interest and helps the eye move across the quilt, adding intrigue. Think of those first few favorites you placed as beacons, calling your eyes to travel across the quilt surface from top to bottom.

Unifying the visual elements in your quilt, such as fabric pattern and the size of the prints that you use, plays a critical role in adding contrast to your project.

Solids versus Prints

I prefer to design with prints rather than solids. However, it's always good practice to expand one's possibilities, so I included "Drawers" (page 50), which is made using Moda Bella solids. The color palette is expansive and worked well with the images I used for color inspiration. Besides, it was fun to challenge myself to come up with a quilt using only solids—something I rarely do (and something I'd like to continue to explore).

When working with prints, the more diverse the prints are, the more interesting your quilt will be. For instance, selecting a floral, a stylized geometric, and a polka dot will add interest to your project. Consider using a polka dot or small-scale print in a project that calls for a solid, or using a zigzag print for binding.

If you're like me and haven't created many quilts using solids, refer to the suggestions I shared in "Color Inspiration" (page 8). When deciding on a color scheme for "Drawers," I searched my idea file on my computer and gleaned color ideas from images of an outdoor mural and a palette of forecasted colors—colors that are predicted to become popular in the future for a determined amount of time.

Taking a few extra minutes to think outside the box is lots of fun and can turn a great quilt into a dynamic new creation, whether you prefer to work with prints, solids, or a combination of the two.

Example of combining prints

The Odd-Number Rule

When I was a young girl, my mom taught me the odd number rule of design. She brought some flowers and greenery in from the garden and showed me how an arrangement looked with two flowers, and then showed me one using three flowers. The arrangement with three flowers was much more visually interesting. Keep this rule in mind when selecting fabrics for your quilts. There are many ways you can incorporate this rule:

- Select three different sizes of prints.
- Select three different color families.
- Select three different types of prints (such as florals, geometrics, and polka dots).

In addition, using an odd number of blocks per row gives balance in two-block quilts, because you start and end each row with the same block. An odd number of rows adds to the balance of a two-block quilt as well. Odd numbers add dimension and will heighten the appeal of a quilt.

Small-, Medium-, and Large-Scale Prints

The size of the print is important to consider when planning a new quilt project. Varying the scale of prints adds yet another layer of interest to a project. Even if you make a quilt using just polka dots, varying the size of the dots makes your project so much more interesting.

Arrangement with even number of flowers

Same-sized dots can be ho-hum.

Arrangement with odd number of flowers

Use a variety of dot sizes for more interest.

Tips for Adding Interest

Here are a few sure-fire ways to add a bit of zing to your quilts.

There are no rules when it comes to sashing and borders. I like to find unusual fabric to use for sashing; something that brings unexpected interest to a quilt. If you're working on a quilt that calls for a solid color, such as the blocks in "Kindred Spirit" (page 58), you could try using one dark geometric or dot print instead of plum and dark-blue solids for sashing. You wouldn't want the print to compete with the bold fabrics of the blocks, so something subtle would be best. Changing things up can be tricky, but do give it a try with a future project and ask for direction from a trusted friend, if needed.

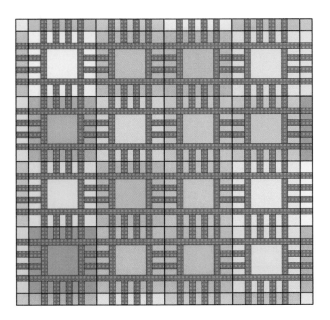

Put thought into your binding. On a scrappy quilt, piece small scraps of the fabrics that make up your quilt top. Zigzags, stripes, or dots add whimsy. Check out other ways to finish the edges, such as a flat-fold or envelope edge.

Update a traditional pattern with unexpected choices. Even though all blocks in a quilt may be the same, make each individual block using different fabrics from your stash. Any that don't work out can be used later in an improvisational or sampler quilt.

Piece scraps together randomly into "yardage." Then, cut certain patches of your blocks from your pieced cloth. Scraps of the pieced cloth can be used later as well.

Use trendy colors. Check out what people are pinning on Pinterest or search online for *fashion trend forecasting* or *trend boards* with the current year in the title. You'll see loads of ideas on combining a marvelous array of current colors.

Before creating each project, think about whether you'd like to work with a collection of fabrics or the fabrics you've collected over time—your stash. Fabric collections typically are well-planned compilations that are coordinated by professional artists. On the contrary, your stash is personal and hand-selected by you, which makes it special and unique.

Collections

I started my career in quilt design by making sample quilts for fabric companies, so it's no wonder that I've continued to enjoy working with fabric collections. The marvelous benefit of working with a collection is that you have a dozen or more fabrics that already complement each other in pattern, scale, and color. Collections have a personality and are easy to use. I used fabric collections for all of the designs in this book and have included the names of the fabrics used for each quilt.

An affordable way to enjoy an entire collection is to purchase precut fabrics. Quilt shops already had fat quarters and fat eighths; Moda added other precuts like the Jelly Roll, Layer Cake, Honey Bun, Dessert Roll, Honeycomb, Mini Charm, Turnover, and Scrap Bag as well. So cool!

I have so many favorite fabric designers that I don't have enough room to list them all. However, there are some fabric designers who I feel step out of the box and show unusual creativity through their eclectic collections. I'm a huge fan of designers such as Amy Butler, Anna Maria Horner, and Kaffe Fassett for their use of color, pattern, and harmonic style. Their fabrics reflect their eclectic styles and, therefore, challenge me.

Assorted precuts

I find such pleasure in working with their collections, among many others. But what appeals to me will not appeal to everyone, so visit your local quilt shop or various fabric manufacturers' websites and take note of the fabric *you* connect with.

For interest, add fabrics from your personal stash to enhance the variety of a collection. Doing this will help you gain confidence in knowing what blends together and will stretch your creativity.

Your Stash

Your stash can be an eclectic array of your personality with no solid plan, or a structured compilation of fabrics for projects you plan to make.

Adding organization to your stash will allow you to see what you have in a pleasing manner. Have you ever heard of *Roy G. Biv?* It's an acronym for sequencing hues in rainbow order: **r**ed, **o**range, **y**ellow, **g**reen, **b**lue, **i**ndigo, and **v**iolet. It's also a great way to organize your stash for quickly locating fabrics by color. As an aside, I do like to keep a collection together if I'm using it for a planned project.

Mix precuts with stash fabrics.

A selection of fat quarters from my stash

Some people know what they like and can make decisions on a dime (lucky them!). I tend to like many different things which sometimes makes it difficult to make decisions on a *personal* level.

One way to discover your unique design style is by creating a mood board. A mood board is a place to gather images that convey a style, feeling, or concept. Designers use them to share their design concepts. They may do so with their colleagues and even clients to convey their vision.

To help you discover your style, collect images of things you enjoy, colors that make you sing, and words and text that describe how you see yourself (confident, powerful, reserved, free spirited, etc.). Combine these elements into a collage and you may be surprised to see what makes up your unique personality.

Whether you use computer software to create a mood board, or simply cut out images from magazines and attach them to a piece of poster board, visually displaying who you are and what you're personally drawn to can bring loads of inspiration. A mood board is essentially a visual reflection of what makes up you; who you are, what you love, what makes you smile, and what brings you joy.

I created a digital mood board through a class exercise. Although I felt confident I knew my tastes, both creating and seeing the finished result excited me about what I liked and how it all stemmed from my love of fine art and nature. Through this process, you can discover your unique likes, too!

Consider the following questions as you compile materials and images for your mood board:

- **What adjectives would you use to describe yourself?** Keep the words positive and uplifting. Try to recognize your strengths through others' eyes. This part of the exercise allows you to appreciate who you are at the core.

- **What brings you joy?** This can truly be anything; no rules apply and it's something that belongs to you and no one else.

- **What colors make you happy?** Select 16 colors that bring you joy. Take your time and come up with an explanation for how each color or group of colors affects you.

- **What fabrics are you drawn to?** Add 16 fabric swatches that you feel are pretty.

- **What are you proud of?** Include images of your quilts or other creations.

- **What else do you love?** The other images on my board show my love of Italian Renaissance art, as well as photos of a forest and pretty flowers. Include what you like.

There's no wrong way of doing this exercise. I would encourage you to use my mood board as a template. However, feel free to further explore and add even more elements to your board!

Mood board

Treble and Bass

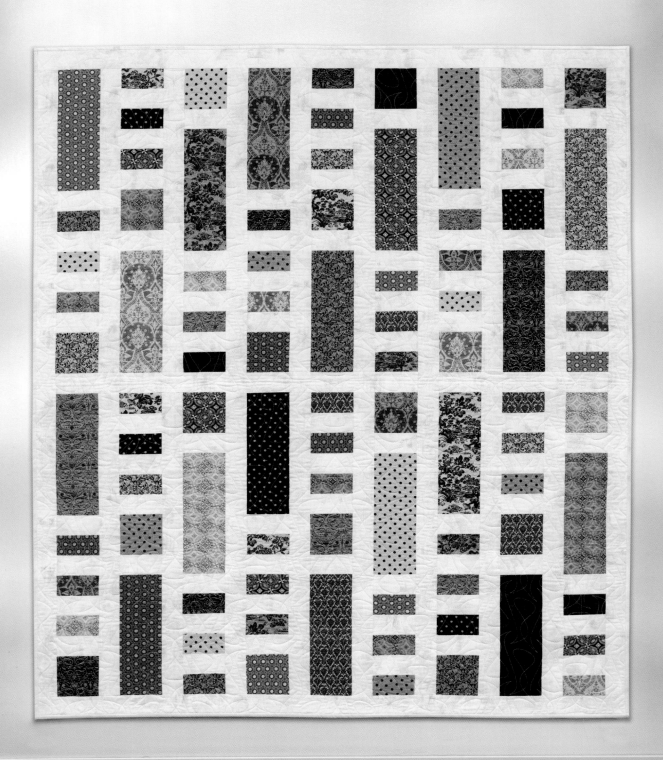

hen I was a young girl, my grandmother bought us a stereo with a turntable and 8-track player. This quilt design reminds me of that stereo, with its rectangular knobs for controlling the treble and bass. I was reminded, too, of how a high-school friend's custom car stereo had panels of small, rectangular lights that would dance to the beat of the music. Good Memories!

"Treble and Bass," pieced by Susan Guzman and machine quilted by Linda Barrett	**Finished quilt:** 56½" x 66½" **Finished blocks:** 16" x 30"

The FABRICS

For this quilt, I used fabrics from the Little Black Dress 2 collection by Basic Grey for Moda. I love the classic design of this collection. It delivers interest with dots, florals, a toile, and timeless prints.

Materials

This pattern is written with directional fabrics in mind so that your prints will be upright. Yardage is based on 42"-wide fabric, unless otherwise noted.

18 fat quarters of assorted cream, gray, and black prints for blocks

3 yards of mottled cream print for blocks, sashing, borders, and binding

4⅛ yards of fabric for backing

66" x 76" piece of batting

Cutting

From the *lengthwise grain* of *each* assorted fat quarter, cut:
  2 strips, 4½" x 18"; crosscut into:
    1 rectangle, 4½" x 12½" (A)
    3 rectangles, 2½" x 4½" (B)
    1 square, 4½" x 4½" (C)

From the *lengthwise grain* of the mottled cream print, cut:
  16 strips, 2½" x 62½"; crosscut *12 of the strips* into:
    2 strips, 2½" x 56½"
    12 strips, 2½" x 30½" (E)
    3 strips, 2½" x 16½" (F)
    39 rectangles, 2½" x 4½" (D)

From the *crosswise grain* of the remaining mottled cream print, cut:
  5 strips, 2½" x 42"; crosscut into 33 rectangles, 2½" x 4½" (D)
  7 strips, 2¼" x 42"

Assembling the Quilt Top

For each block, you'll need three assorted A rectangles, nine assorted B rectangles, and three assorted C squares. You'll also need 12 cream D rectangles and two cream E rectangles.

1. Lay out the A, B, C, and D pieces in three vertical rows as shown on page 20. Join the pieces into rows and press the seam allowances away from the D rectangles. Sew the rows and E pieces together to complete

one block. Press the seam allowances toward the E pieces. Make a total of six blocks.

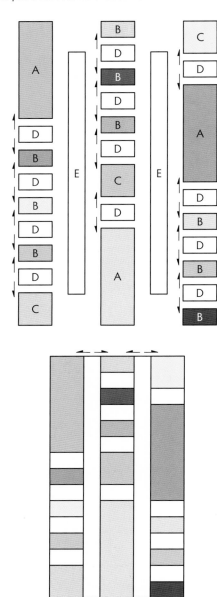

Make 6.

2. Join the blocks and cream F strips as shown, right, to make three vertical rows. Press the seam allowances toward the F strips. Sew the rows and two cream 62½"-long strips together to make the quilt-top center. Press the seam allowances toward the cream strips. The quilt-top center should measure 52½" x 62½".

This pattern is perfect for showcasing medium- and large-scale prints.

3. Sew cream 62½"-long strips to opposite sides of the quilt top. Press the seam allowances toward the cream strips. Sew cream 56½"-long strips to the top and bottom of the quilt top to complete the border. Press the seam allowances toward the cream strips.

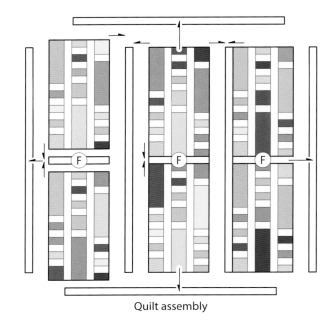

Quilt assembly

Finishing

1. Cut the backing fabric into two equal lengths and remove the selvage edges. Sew the lengths together and trim the sides to make a 66" x 76" backing.

2. Layer and baste the backing, batting, and quilt top. Quilt as desired.

3. Referring to "Binding Your Quilt" (page 76) and using the cream 2¼"-wide strips, make and attach binding. Make a label with your name, date, and thoughtful message to the receiver; sew it to the back of the quilt to finish.

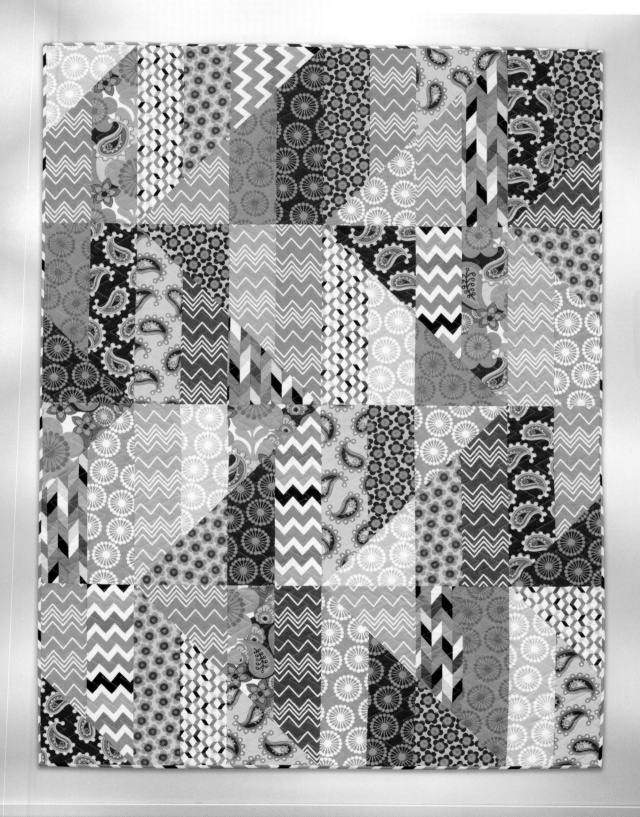

A crooked path is so much more interesting than one that's straight—you never know what intriguing adventure lies right around the corner! This oversized zigzag design accommodates large-scale prints beautifully, due to the generous patches you'll cut.

"Crooked Path," pieced by Susan Guzman and machine quilted by Linda Barrett

Finished quilt: 60½" x 80½"
Finished blocks: 10" x 20"

The FABRICS

Whether you prefer bright colors or a more muted palette, choose large prints that make *you* swoon! Be sure to add interesting contrast, such as florals with geometric prints. For this quilt, I used fabrics from two collections by French Bull for Windham Fabrics.

Materials

This pattern is written with directional prints in mind. However, it works whether you choose directional or allover prints. Yardage is based on 42"-wide fabric, unless otherwise noted.

1¼ yards of multicolored zigzag print for blocks and binding

⅔ yard *each* of 15 coordinating large-scale blue, white, orange, pink, purple, yellow, green, gray, and black prints for blocks

5¼ yards of fabric for backing

70" x 90" piece of batting

Cutting

From the *lengthwise grain* of *each of 8* coordinating prints, cut:
    3 rectangles, 5½" x 20½" (24 total; A)
    2 squares, 10½" x 10½" (16 total; B)

From the *lengthwise grain* of *each of the remaining* 7 coordinating prints, cut:
    3 rectangles, 5½" x 20½" (21 total; A)
    1 square, 10½" x 10½" (7 total; B)

From the multicolored zigzag print, cut:
    3 rectangles, 5½" x 20½" (A)
    1 square, 10½" x 10½" (B)
    8 strips, 2¼" x 42"

Assembling the Quilt Top

For each block, you'll need two different A rectangles and one B square.

1. Sew two A rectangles together to make a rectangular unit. Press the seam allowance in one direction. Make a total of 24 units.

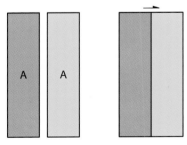

Make 24.

2. Mark a diagonal line from corner to corner on the wrong side of a B square. Place the marked square on one unit as shown, right sides together. Sew along the marked line. Trim away the corner fabric, leaving a ¼" seam allowance. Press the resulting triangle

open. Make a total of six blocks. Save the leftover triangles to use in another project, or piece them together and incorporate the pieces into the backing.

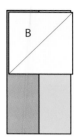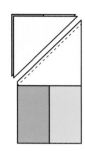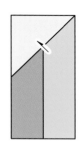

Make 6.

3. Repeat steps 1 and 2 to make six of each block as shown.

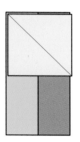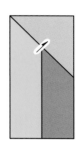

Make 6.

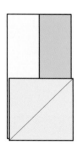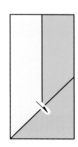

Make 6.

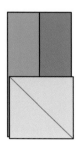

Make 6.

A secondary chevron pattern emerges when triangles align as blocks are joined.

4. Lay out the blocks in four rows of six blocks each, making sure to orient them as shown in the quilt assembly diagram. Sew the blocks together into rows. Press the seam allowances in opposite directions from row to row. Join the rows and press the seam allowances in one direction.

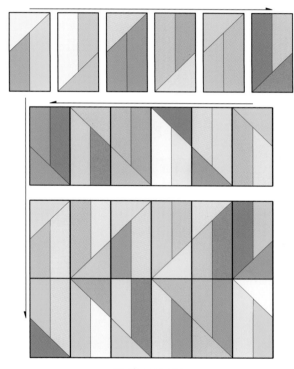

Quilt assembly

Finishing

1. Cut the backing fabric into two equal lengths and remove the selvage edges. Sew the lengths together and trim the sides to make a 70" x 90" backing.

2. Layer and baste the backing, batting, and quilt top. Quilt as desired.

3. Referring to "Binding Your Quilt" (page 76) and using the multicolored zigzag print strips, make and attach binding. Make a label with your name, date, and thoughtful message to the receiver; sew to the back of the quilt to finish.

This versatile design works well with different fabric styles and colorways. Does the path lead out or in? Whichever way you're going, may your journey be ever changing, exciting, and satisfying to the soul!

"Journeys," pieced by Susan Guzman and machine quilted by Linda Barrett	**Finished quilt:** 68½" x 84½" **Finished blocks:** 14" x 18"

The FABRICS

David Butler's Parson Gray fabrics for FreeSpirit are uncluttered, serene, and contemporary, like the Asian design aesthetic I adore. This collection is called World Tour.

Materials

Yardage is based on 42"-wide fabric, unless otherwise noted.

2⅝ yards of gray print for blocks, sashing, and border

2 yards of blue print for blocks, sashing, border, and binding

1⅝ yards of ivory print for blocks*

1⅜ yards of navy print for blocks*

5½ yards of fabric for backing

78" x 94" piece of batting

*I used utility linen in place of 100% cotton for these fabrics.

Cutting

From the gray print, cut:
   33 strips, 2½" x 42"; crosscut into:
     24 rectangles, 2½" x 4½" (A)
     24 rectangles, 2½" x 8½" (B)
     24 rectangles, 2½" x 12½" (C)
     4 rectangles, 2½" x 14½" (E)
     4 rectangles, 2½" x 16½" (D)
     4 strips, 2½" x 32½" (F)
     2 strips, 2½" x 34½" (G)
     4 strips, 2½" x 36½" (H)
     2 strips, 2½" x 40½" (I)

From the navy print, cut:
   16 strips, 2½" x 42"; crosscut into:
     16 rectangles, 2½" x 4½" (A)
     16 rectangles, 2½" x 8½" (B)
     16 rectangles, 2½" x 12½" (C)
     4 rectangles, 2½" x 14½" (E)
     4 rectangles, 2½" x 16½" (D)

From the ivory print, cut:
   20 strips, 2½" x 42"; crosscut into:
     16 rectangles, 2½" x 4½" (A)
     16 rectangles, 2½" x 8½" (B)
     16 rectangles, 2½" x 12½" (C)
     8 rectangles, 2½" x 14½" (E)
     8 rectangles, 2½" x 16½" (D)

From the blue print, cut:
   18 strips, 2½" x 42"; crosscut into:
     8 rectangles, 2½" x 4½" (A)
     8 rectangles, 2½" x 8½" (B)
     8 rectangles, 2½" x 12½" (C)
     4 strips, 2½" x 32½" (F)
     2 strips, 2½" x 34½" (G)
     4 strips, 2½" x 36½" (H)
     2 strips, 2½" x 40½" (I)
   8 strips, 2¼" x 42"

Assembling the Blocks

After sewing each seam, press the seam allowances in the directions indicated.

1. Sew a gray A rectangle to the long side of a navy A rectangle. Sew a navy A rectangle to the top of the unit and a gray A rectangle to the bottom of the unit as shown. Make a total of four units.

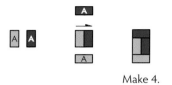

Make 4.

2. Sew a gray B rectangle to the right side of a unit from step 1 and a navy B rectangle to the left side of the unit as shown. Then sew gray and navy B rectangles to the top and bottom of the unit as shown. Make a total of four units.

Make 4.

3. Sew a navy C rectangle to the right side of a unit from step 2 and a gray C rectangle to the left side of the unit as shown. Then sew navy and gray C rectangles to the top and bottom of the unit as shown. Make a total of four units.

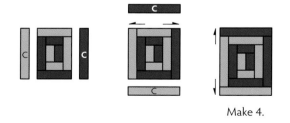

Make 4.

4. Sew a gray D rectangle to the right side of the unit. Sew a gray E rectangle to the top of the unit to complete the block. Make a total of four of block 1.

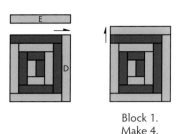

Block 1.
Make 4.

5. Repeat step 1–4 to make a total of four of block 3, making sure to reverse the positions of the gray and navy rectangles.

Block 3.
Make 4.

6. Repeat steps 1–3 using the ivory A, B, and C rectangles and the blue A, B, and C rectangles to make four units. Then sew an ivory D rectangle to the left side of each unit and an ivory E rectangle to the top of each unit to make four of block 2.

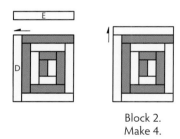

Block 2.
Make 4.

7. Repeat steps 1–3, using the ivory A, B, and C rectangles and the remaining gray A, B, and C rectangles to make four units. Then sew an ivory D rectangle to the left side of each unit and an ivory E rectangle to the top of each unit to make four of block 4.

Block 4.
Make 4.

Assembling the Quilt Top

1. Lay out two of block 1 and two of block 2 in two rows, making sure to rotate the blocks in the bottom row. Join the blocks into rows. Press the seam allowances toward block 1. Join the rows to complete the section and press the seam allowances in one direction. Make two sections.

2. Sew the blue H strips to opposite sides of each section from step 1. Then sew the blue F strips to the top and bottom of the section. Add a gray I strip to the left side and a gray G strip to the top of the section. Press all seam allowances toward the just-added strips. Repeat to make a second identical section.

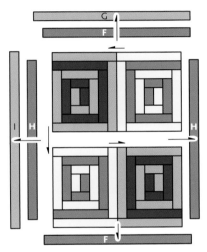

Make 2.

3. Repeat steps 1 and 2 using blocks 3 and 4, the gray F and H strips, and the blue I and G strips to make two sections.

Make 2.

> *A basic labyrinth has a single, non-branching path which leads to its center.*

4. Lay out the sections as shown in the quilt assembly diagram below. Join the sections into rows. Press the seam allowances in opposite directions from row to row. Join the rows and press the seam allowances in one direction.

Quilt assembly

Finishing

1. Cut the backing fabric into two equal lengths and remove the selvage edges. Sew the lengths together and trim the sides to make a 78" x 94" backing.

2. Layer and baste the backing, batting, and quilt top. Quilt as desired.

3. Referring to "Binding Your Quilt" (page 76) and using the blue 2¼"-wide strips, make and attach binding. Make a label with your name, date, and thoughtful message to the receiver, and sew to the back of the quilt to finish.

Bookshelves

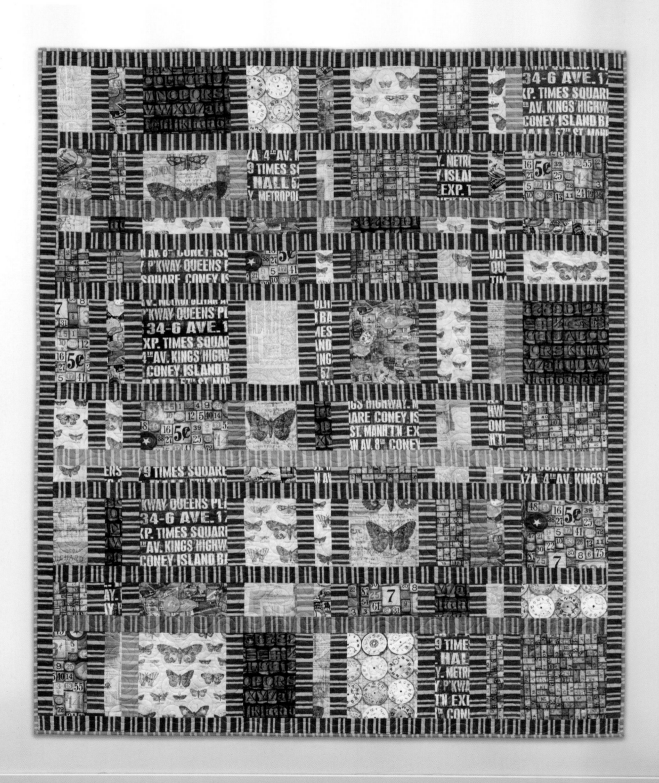

*W*hile paging through an interior-design magazine, I came across a photo that showed an interesting wall of bookshelves in a contemporary setting. Because of my love of reading, the image inspired me to design a quilt that reminded me of those shelves. The fabric I used gives my quilt a "cabinet of curiosities" feel.

"Bookshelves," pieced and machine quilted by Linda Barrett	Finished quilt: 68½" x 82½"

The FABRICS

This scrappy quilt has a lot of versatility. I've made it with 1940s prints as well as a fresh, modern fabric collection. Here, I used the first collection by designer Tim Holtz, called Eclectic Elements for Coats and Clark.

Materials

Yardage is based on 42"-wide fabric, unless otherwise noted and is suitable for directional prints.

15 fat quarters of assorted red, cream, gray, brown, black, green, blue, and yellow prints for rectangles

1⅔ yards of brown stripe for sashing and borders

⅞ yard of red stripe for sashing and binding

½ yard of blue stripe for sashing

5⅜ yards of backing fabric

78" x 92" piece of batting

Cutting

From the assorted fat quarters, cut *a total of:**
6 squares, 2½" x 2½" (A)
4 squares, 4½" x 4½" (B)
2 squares, 6½" x 6½" (C)
2 squares, 8½" x 8½" (D)
4 squares, 10½" x 10½" (E)
10 rectangles, 2½" x 4½" (F)

8 rectangles, 2½" x 6½" (G)
8 rectangles, 2½" x 8½" (H)
10 rectangles, 2½" x 10½" (I)
6 rectangles, 4½" x 6½" (J)
6 rectangles, 4½" x 8½" (K)
8 rectangles, 4½" x 10½" (L)
4 rectangles, 6½" x 8½" (M)
6 rectangles, 6½" x 10½" (N)
6 rectangles, 8½" x 10½" (O)

From the brown stripe, cut:
33 strips, 2½" x 42"; cut *15 of the strips* into:
    14 squares, 2½" x 2½" (P)
    14 rectangles, 2½" x 4½" (Q)
    14 rectangles, 2½" x 6½" (R)
    14 rectangles, 2½" x 8½" (S)
    14 rectangles, 2½" x 10½" (T)

From the blue stripe, cut:
5 strips, 2½" x 42"; cut *1 of the strips* into:
    1 square, 2½" x 2½" (P)
    1 rectangle, 2½" x 4½" (Q)
    1 rectangle, 2½" x 6½" (R)
    1 rectangle, 2½" x 8½" (S)
    1 rectangle, 2½" x 10½" (T)

From the red stripe, cut:
3 strips, 2½" x 42"; cut *1 of the strips* into:
    1 square, 2½" x 2½" (P)
    1 rectangle, 2½" x 4½" (Q)
    1 rectangle, 2½" x 6½" (R)
    1 rectangle, 2½" x 8½" (S)
    1 rectangle, 2½" x 10½" (T)
8 strips, 2¼" x 42"

*Pay careful attention to the orientation of fabric, referring to the photo (page 28) as needed.

Assembling the Quilt Top

1. Lay out the print A–O squares and rectangles, brown rectangles, red rectangles, and blue rectangles in rows as shown, paying attention to the orientation of the pieces. (Note that the illustration is rotated 90°; the top row is on right.) Join the pieces into rows. Press the seam allowances in the directions indicated. Make two of each row.

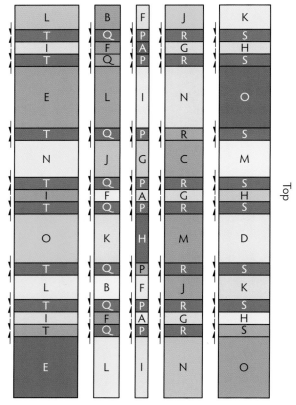

Make 2 of each.

2. Join 10 brown strips end to end. From the pieced strip, cut six 64½"-long sashing strips. Join the remaining blue strips end to end and cut two 64½"-long sashing strips. Join the remaining red 2½"-long strips end to end and cut one 64½"-long sashing strip.

3. Join the block rows and sashing strips from step 2 as shown in the quilt assembly diagram, right, to complete the quilt center. Press the seam allowances toward the sashing strips. The quilt center should measure 64½" x 78½".

4. Join the remaining brown strips end to end. From the pieced strip, cut two 78½"-long

Reimagine this quilt in solids for a make-your-own plaid look.

sashing strips. Sew the strips to opposite sides of the quilt center. Press the seam allowances toward the brown strips.

5. From the remaining pieced strip, cut two 68½"-long strips and sew them to the top and bottom of the quilt top to complete the border. Press the seam allowances toward the brown strips.

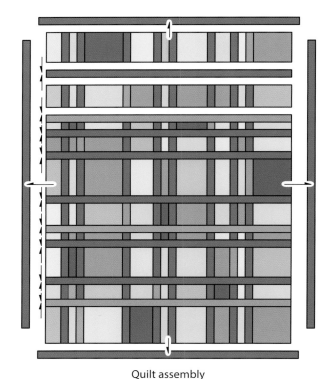

Quilt assembly

Finishing

1. Cut the backing fabric into two equal lengths and remove the selvage edges. Sew the lengths together and trim the sides to make a 78" x 82" backing.

2. Layer and baste the backing, batting, and quilt top. Quilt as desired.

3. Referring to "Binding Your Quilt" (page 76) and using the red 2¼"-wide strips, make and attach binding. Make a label with your name, date, and thoughtful message to the receiver; sew to the back of the quilt to finish.

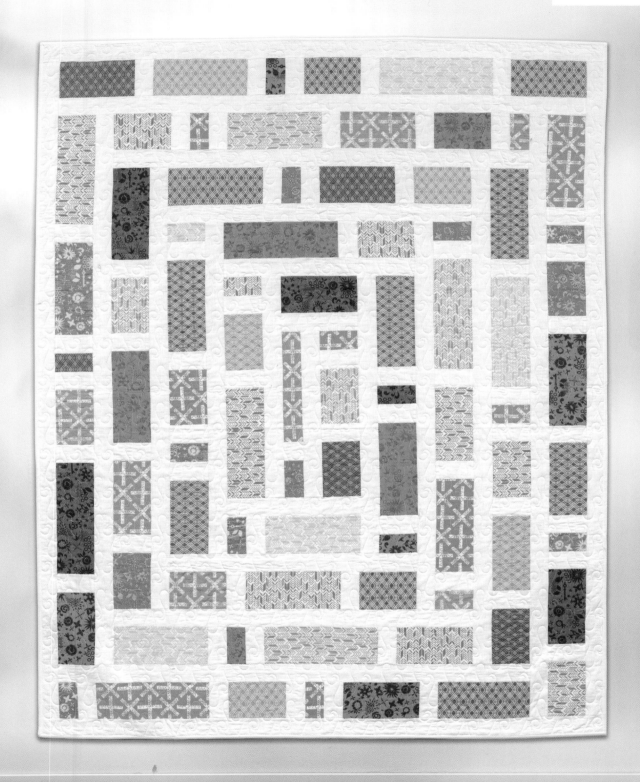

*T*his design is my modern take on a Log Cabin block, where each "log" is surrounded by sashing. As with the traditional block, piecing begins in the center. Being organized is important with this quilt because of all of the different-sized strips. Labeling each patch and strip you cut is paramount to worry-free piecing.

"Jazz," pieced and machine quilted by Linda Barrett	Finished quilt: 60½" x 76½"

The FABRICS

I fell in love with the bright, saturated colors of Alison Glass's fabric for Andover Fabrics and wanted to come up with a design that allowed the fabrics to jive. This cheerful quilt brings to mind a summertime Jazz festival.

Materials

Yardage is based on 42"-wide fabric, unless otherwise noted.

16 fat quarters of assorted orange, purple, blue, green, red, yellow, and pink prints for rectangles

3⅜ yards of white solid for sashing, outer border, and binding

5 yards of fabric for backing

70" x 86" piece of batting

Cutting

From the assorted fat quarters, cut *a total of:*
  1 rectangle, 2½" x 12½" (A)
  9 rectangles, 4½" x 12½" (E)
  17 rectangles, 4½" x 10½" (F)
  14 rectangles, 4½" x 8½" (D)
  19 rectangles, 4½" x 6½" (C)
  21 rectangles, 2½" x 4½" (B)

From the *lengthwise grain* of the white solid, cut:
  16 strips, 2½" x 72½"; cut *14 of the strips* into:
    1 strip, 2½" x 66½" (Z)
    3 strips, 2½" x 60½" (Y)
    1 strip, 2½" x 56½" (X)
    1 strip, 2½" x 54½" (W)
    1 strip, 2½" x 50½" (V)
    1 strip, 2½" x 48½" (U)
    1 strip, 2½" x 44½" (T)
    1 square, 2½" x 2½" (G)
    1 rectangle, 2½" x 8½" (J)
    1 strip, 2½" x 14½" (K)
    1 strip, 2½" x 42½" (S)
    1 strip, 2½" x 18½" (H)
    1 strip, 2½" x 38½" (R)
    1 strip, 2½" x 20½" (L)
    1 strip, 2½" x 36½" (Q)
    1 strip, 2½" x 24½" (M)
    1 strip, 2½" x 32½" (P)
    1 strip, 2½" x 26½" (N)
    1 strip, 2½" x 30½" (O)

From the *crosswise grain* of the remaining white solid, cut:
  4 strips, 4½" x 42"; crosscut into 61 rectangles, 2½" x 4½" (I)
  8 strips, 2¼" x 42"

Cheerful colors bring to mind a summertime jazz festival.

Assembling the Quilt Top

Lay out the print A–F rectangles, the white G square, and the white H–Z rectangles as shown in the quilt assembly diagram on page 34.

1. Join the pieces into units, starting in the center of the quilt top with the print A rectangle, the white G square, and a print B rectangle. Press the seam allowances toward the A and B rectangles. Sew the white H strip to the right side of the row. Press the seam allowances toward the H strip.

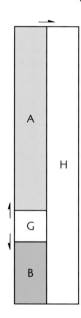

2. Join one print B rectangle, two white I rectangles, and two print C rectangles to make a unit. Press the seam allowances toward the B and C rectangles. Sew the row

to the other side of the H strip and press the seam allowances toward H.

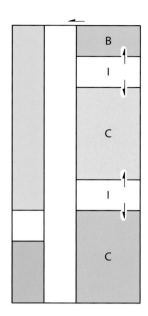

3. Sew the white J rectangle and a print D rectangle to the top of the unit from step 2. Press the seam allowances toward the just-added rectangles. Sew the white M strip to the left side of the unit and press.

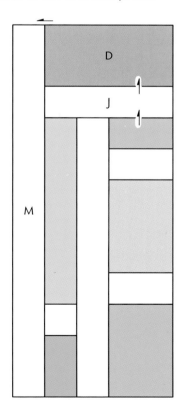

4. Continue in the same way, joining the rectangles into units, and then sewing the units and white strips to the center unit as shown in the quilt assembly diagram. The quilt center should measure 56½" x 72½".

5. Sew the remaining white 72½"-long strips to opposite sides of the quilt center. Press the seam allowances toward the white strips. Sew the remaining Y strips to the top and bottom of the quilt top to complete the border. Press the seam allowances toward the white strips.

Finishing

1. Cut the backing fabric into two equal lengths and remove the selvage edges. Sew the lengths together and trim the sides to make a 70" x 86" backing.

2. Layer and baste the backing, batting, and quilt top. Quilt as desired.

3. Referring to "Binding Your Quilt" (page 76) and using the white 2¼"-wide strips, make and attach binding. Make a label with your name, date, and thoughtful message to the receiver; sew it to the back of the quilt to finish.

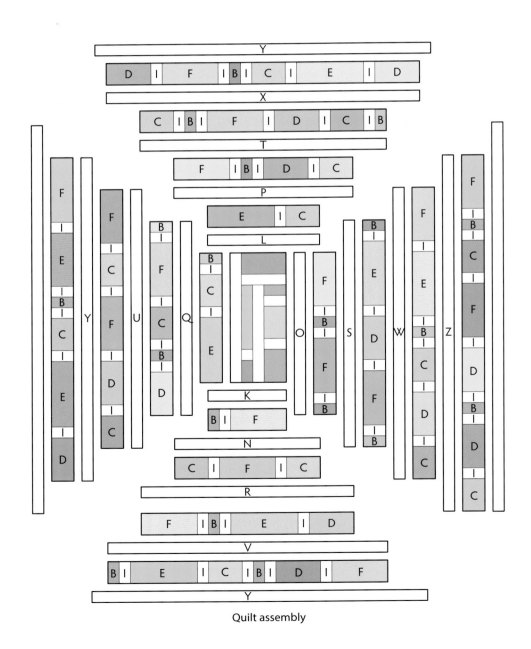

Quilt assembly

*T*he inspiration for this split-octagon design came from a fashion magazine. As the design evolved, I added a lone Double Triangle block as a point of interest. Then I decided to add a block to each row in order to make the design cohesive and add a visual rhythm through random placement.

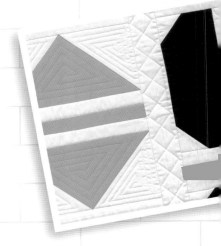

"Rogue," pieced and machine quilted by Linda Barrett

Finished quilt: 74½" x 73½"
Finished Octagon blocks: 10" x 10"
Finished Double Triangle blocks: 10" x 13"

The FABRICS

I used Pure Elements solids by Art Gallery Fabrics. The solid colors and simple, clean block designs are reminiscent of those found in nautical flags.

Materials

Yardage is based on 42"-wide fabric, unless otherwise noted.

4⅝ yards of ivory solid for blocks, sashing, border, and binding

2⅝ yards of navy solid for blocks and sashing

⅞ yard of orange solid for blocks

7¼ yards of fabric for backing

83" x 84" piece of batting

Cutting

From the *lengthwise grain* of the ivory solid, cut:
13 strips, 2½" x 74½"; cut *11 of the strips* into:
7 strips, 2½" x 69½"
24 rectangles, 2½" x 10½" (C)
4 strips, 1½" x 74½"; crosscut into 28 rectangles, 1½" x 10½" (F)

From the *crosswise grain* of the remaining ivory solid, cut:
2 strips, 10½" x 42"; crosscut into 44 rectangles, 1½" x 10½" (F)
4 strips, 5½" x 42"; crosscut into 24 squares, 5½" x 5½" (E)
6 strips, 2½" x 42"; crosscut into 96 squares, 2½" x 2½" (B)
8 strips, 2¼" x 42"

From the navy solid, cut:
8 strips, 10½" x 42"; crosscut into:
48 rectangles, 4½" x 10½" (A)
36 rectangles, 1½" x 10½" (G)

From the orange solid, cut:
2 strips, 10½" x 42"; crosscut into 12 rectangles, 5½" x 10½" (D)
2 strips, 1½" x 42"; crosscut into 6 rectangles, 1½" x 10½" (H)

Assembling the Octagon Blocks

1. Draw a diagonal line from corner to corner on the wrong side of each ivory B square. Layer marked squares on two corners of a navy A rectangle. Sew along the marked lines. Trim away the corner fabric, leaving a ¼" seam

allowance. Press the seam allowances toward the resulting triangles. Make a total of 48 units.

Make 48.

2. Join two units from step 1 and one ivory C rectangle as shown to make an octagon block. Press the seam allowances toward the C rectangle. Make a total of 24 blocks.

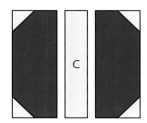

Make 24.

Assembling the Double Triangle Blocks

1. Draw a diagonal line from corner to corner on the wrong side of each ivory E square. Place a marked square on one end of an orange D rectangle. Sew along the marked line. Trim away the corner fabric, leaving a ¼" seam allowance. Press the seam allowances toward the resulting ivory triangle. Place a marked square on the opposite end of the rectangle. Sew, trim, and press to make one flying-geese unit. Make a total of 12 units.

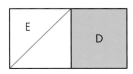
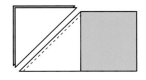
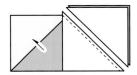
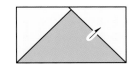

Make 12.

> *Want a more playful quilt? Choose primary colors for a croquet ball look.*

2. Join two ivory F rectangles and one orange G rectangle to make a strip unit. Make a total of six units. Press the seam allowances toward the G rectangle.

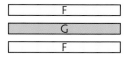

Make 6.

3. Sew together two flying-geese units and one strip unit as shown to make one block. Press the seam allowances toward the center. Make a total of six blocks.

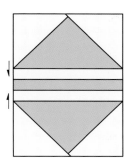
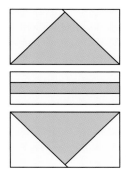

Make 6.

Tip | Change It Up

Use a cherry-red solid instead of orange for a patriotic look. Or, use your alma mater's colors. Take it a step further and use two small-scale prints instead of the navy and orange solids. For the background, add a colorful, coordinating solid for interest.

Assembling the Quilt Top

1. Sew an ivory F rectangle to one long edge of a navy H rectangle to make a two-strip sashing unit. Press the seam allowances toward the H rectangle. Make 12 units.

Make 12.

2. Sew ivory F rectangles to both long edges of a navy H rectangle to make a three-strip sashing unit. Press the seam allowances toward the H rectangle. Make 24 units.

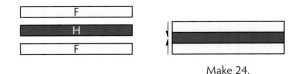

Make 24.

3. Lay out four Octagon blocks, one Double Triangle block, two two-strip sashing units, and four three-strip units as shown in the quilt assembly diagram, right. Join the blocks and sashing units to make a vertical row. Press the seam allowances toward the sashing units. The row should measure 69½" long. Paying attention to block orientation, make a total of six rows.

4. Lay out the vertical rows and five ivory 69½"-long strips as shown in the quilt assembly diagram. Join the rows and strips to complete the quilt center. Press the seam allowances toward the ivory strips. The quilt center should measure 69½" x 70½".

5. Sew ivory 69½"-long strips to opposite sides of the quilt top. Press the seam allowances toward the ivory strips. Sew ivory 74½"-long

strips to the top and bottom of the quilt top to complete the border. Press the seam allowances toward the ivory strips.

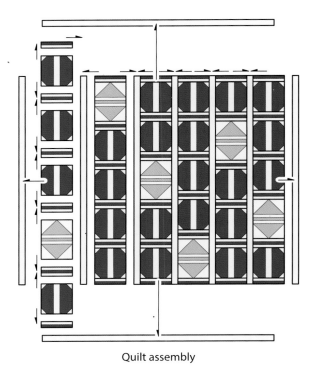

Quilt assembly

Finishing

1. Cut the backing fabric into three equal lengths and remove the selvage edges. Sew the lengths together and trim the sides to make an 83" x 84" backing.

2. Layer and baste the backing, batting, and quilt top. Quilt as desired.

3. Referring to "Binding Your Quilt" (page 76) and using the ivory 2¼"-wide strips, make and attach binding. Make a label with your name, date, and thoughtful message to the receiver; sew to the back of the quilt to finish.

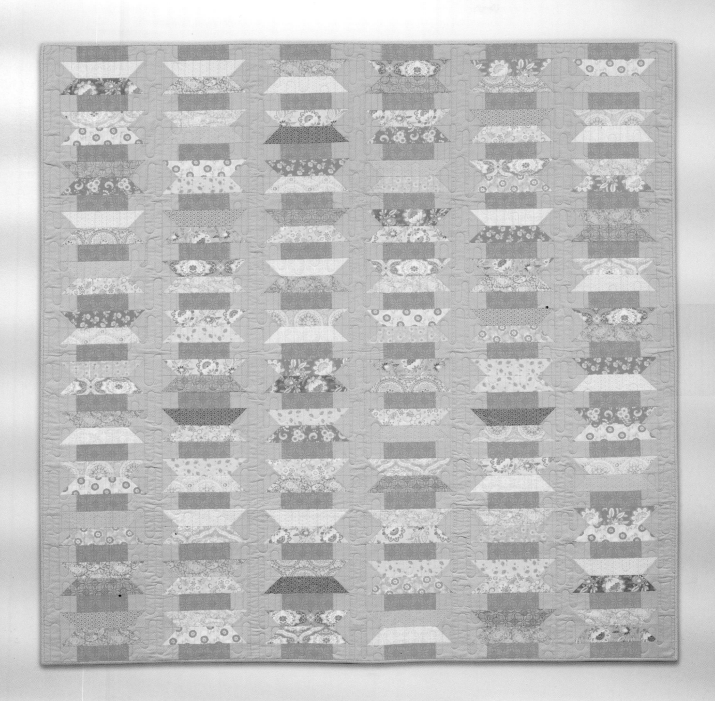

This design has been in my sketchbook for a long time. My goal was to use a Jelly Roll in a unique way, keeping the design simple enough that you could make the quilt fairly quickly. I feel I've accomplished this goal and hope you'll enjoy making this quilt as much as I have!

"Flair," pieced by Susan Guzman and machine quilted by Linda Barrett

Finished quilt: 74" x 74½"
Finished blocks: 4" x 10"

The FABRICS

The pretty prints in this quilt are from the High Street collection by Lily Ashbury for Moda. I love how Lily combines such pretty colors with her fresh, classic designs. The colors appear to pop off the gray-solid background.

Materials

Yardage is based on 42"-wide fabric, unless otherwise noted.

3⅛ yards of gray solid for blocks and sashing

36 strips, 2½" x 42", of assorted prints for blocks

1 yard of orange print for sashing

⅝ yard of pink print for binding

7⅜ yards of fabric for backing*

84" x 84" piece of batting

If backing fabric is 42" wide after washing, you'll need 5 yards.

Cutting

Before trimming selvages from the assorted print strips, make sure you have at least 42" of usable print.

From *each* assorted print strip, cut:
  4 rectangles, 2½" x 10½" (144 total; A)

From the orange print, cut:
  5 strips, 6½" x 42"; crosscut into 78 rectangles, 2½" x 6½" (B)

From the *lengthwise grain* of the gray solid, cut:
  16 strips, 2½" x 74½"; crosscut *9 of the strips* into 261 squares, 2½" x 2½" (C)

From the *crosswise grain* of the remaining gray solid, cut:
  12 strips, 2½" x 42"; crosscut into 183 squares, 2½" x 2½" (C)

From the pink print, cut:
  8 strips, 2¼" x 42"

Assembling the Quilt Top

1. Sew together one orange B rectangle and two gray C squares as shown to make a sashing unit. Make a total of 78 units.

Make 78.

> *Show off your flair for fabric, using your favorite Jelly Roll.*

2. Draw a diagonal line from corner to corner on the wrong side of each remaining gray C square. Place a marked square on one end of a print A rectangle. Sew along the marked line. Trim away the corner fabric, leaving a ¼" seam allowance. Press the seam allowances toward the resulting gray triangle. Place a marked square on the opposite end of the rectangle. Sew, trim, and press to make one unit. Make a total of 144 units.

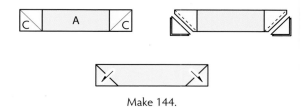

Make 144.

3. Sew two units from step 2 together as shown to make a block. Press the seam allowances open. Make a total of 72 blocks.

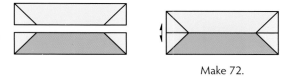

Make 72.

4. Join 13 sashing units and 12 blocks to make a vertical row as shown in the quilt assembly diagram, above right. Press the seam allowances toward the sashing units. The row should measure 74½" long. Make a total of six rows.

| Tip | You Be the Designer |

Select a Jelly Roll that appeals to you, then choose a solid color that appears consistently throughout the collection for the background. The solid will automatically blend with all the prints. Enjoy the creative process!

5. Join the rows and gray 74½"-long strips to complete the quilt top. Press the seam allowances toward the gray strips.

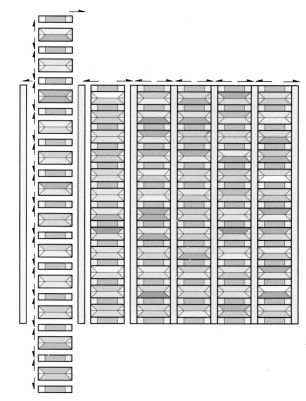

Quilt assembly

Finishing

1. Cut the backing fabric into three equal lengths and remove the selvage edges. Sew the lengths together and trim the sides to make an 84" x 84" backing.

2. Layer and baste the backing, batting, and quilt top. Quilt as desired.

3. Referring to "Binding Your Quilt" (page 76) and using the pink 2¼"-wide strips, make and attach binding. Make a label with your name, date, and thoughtful message to the receiver; sew to the back of the quilt to finish.

Connections

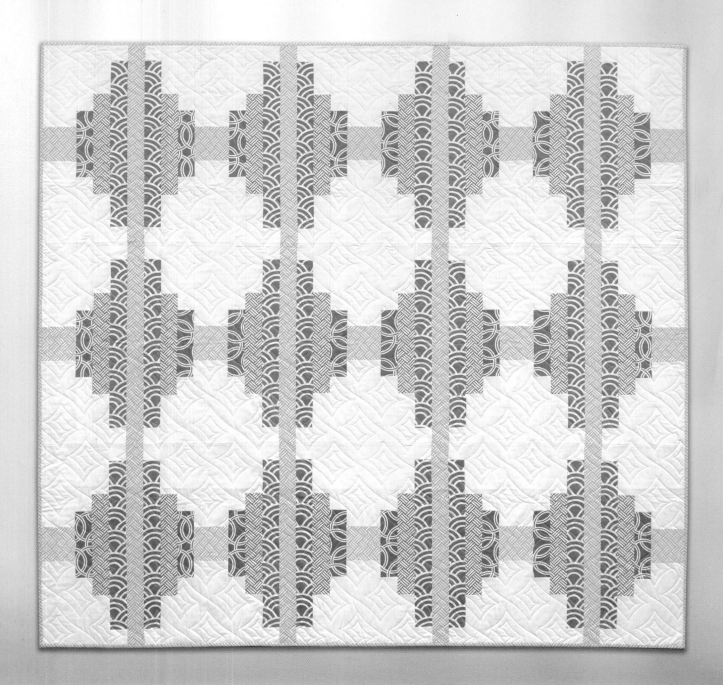

*A*rtful fabric inspired this design. The simple, clean blocks are refreshing against the white background. Because the fabrics are simple two-color prints, the quilt design is uncomplicated as well.

"Connections," pieced and machine quilted by Linda Barrett	Finished quilt: 76½" x 72½" Finished blocks: 14" x 24"

The FABRICS

I fell in love with the bold color and graphic nature of the Bekko collection by Trenna Travis for Michael Miller Fabrics. Although the collection is home-decor fabric, it worked beautifully in this cheery quilt.

Materials

Yardage is based on 42"-wide fabric, unless otherwise noted.

3 yards of white solid for blocks and sashing

1⅜ yards of pink print #1 for blocks

⅞ yard of pink print #2 for blocks

⅝ yard of pink print #3 for blocks

1½ yards of green print for blocks and binding

7 yards of backing fabric

82" x 86" piece of batting

Cutting

From the white solid, cut:
  3 strips, 2½" x 42"; crosscut into 48 squares, 2½" x 2½" (A)
  3 strips, 6½" x 42"; crosscut into 48 rectangles, 2½" x 6½" (C)
  3 strips, 8½" x 42"; crosscut into 48 rectangles, 2½" x 8½" (E)
  4 strips, 10½" x 42"; crosscut into 30 rectangles, 4½" x 10½" (G)

From pink print #1, cut:
  2 strips, 20½" x 42"; crosscut into 24 rectangles, 2½" x 20½" (B)

From pink print #2, cut:
  2 strips, 12½" x 42"; crosscut into 24 rectangles, 2½" x 12½" (D)

From pink print #3, cut:
  2 strips, 8½" x 42"; crosscut into 24 rectangles, 2½" x 8½"(E)

From the green print, cut:
  1 strip, 24½" x 42"; crosscut into:
    12 rectangles, 2½" x 24½" (F)
    10 squares, 4½" x 4½" (H)
  1 strip, 4½" x 42"; crosscut into 5 squares, 4½" x 4½" (H)
  8 strips, 2¼" x 42"

Tip   Color-Palette Change Up

Selecting two bold fabrics for prints #1 and #3, and a more subtle fabric for print #2, breaks up the intensity of the block design. If you prefer a darker color palette, choose three dark fabrics for the pink prints, a medium-value fabric for the green print, and a light small-scale print for the background.

Assembling the Blocks

1. Sew together two white A squares and one pink #1 B rectangle to make a 24½"-long pieced strip. Press the seam allowances toward the pink rectangle. Make a total of 24 pieced strips.

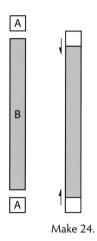

Make 24.

2. Sew together two white C rectangles and one pink #2 D rectangle to make a 24½"-long pieced strip. Press the seam allowances toward the pink rectangle. Make a total of 24 pieced strips.

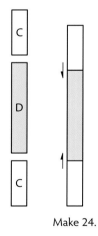

Make 24.

3. Sew together two white E rectangles and one pink #3 E rectangle to make a 24½"-long pieced strip. Press the seam allowances toward the pink rectangle. Make a total of 24 pieced strips.

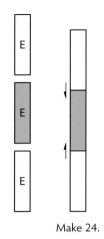

Make 24.

4. Lay out two strips from step 1, two strips from step 2, two strips from step 3, and one green F rectangle. Join the pieces to make one block. Press the seam allowances toward the green rectangle. Make a total of 12 blocks.

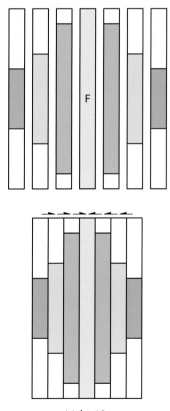

Make 12.

Don't overlook the home dec department when shopping for quilt fabrics.

Assembling the Quilt Top

1. Join two white G rectangles and one green H square to make a sashing unit. Make a total of 15 units.

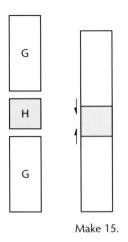

Make 15.

2. Lay out the blocks and sashing units in three rows, alternating the blocks and sashing units as shown in the quilt assembly diagram below. Sew the pieces together into rows. Press the seam allowances in opposite directions from row to row. Sew the rows together to complete the quilt top. Press the seam allowances in one direction.

Finishing

1. Cut the backing fabric into three equal lengths and remove the selvage edges. Sew the lengths together and trim the sides to make an 82" x 86" backing.

2. Layer and baste the backing, batting, and quilt top. Quilt as desired.

3. Referring to "Binding Your Quilt" (page 76) and using the green 2¼"-wide strips, make and attach binding. Make a label with your name, date, and thoughtful message to the receiver; sew to the back of the quilt to finish.

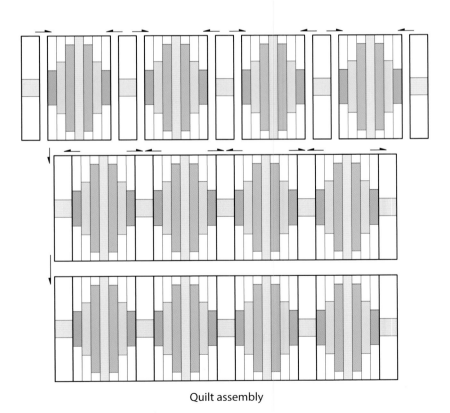

Quilt assembly

Bejeweled

A variety of jewel-tone blocks fill the center of this quilt, while on-point squares make the blocks shimmer. This design is dedicated to all the gems in my life in the form of family and friends. I value and treasure you dearly!

"Bejeweled," pieced and machine quilted by Linda Barrett

Finished quilt: 76½" x 92½"
Finished blocks: vary from 4" x 4" to 4" x 28"

The FABRICS

For this quilt, I used fabrics from Anna Maria Horner's Dowry and True Colors collections for FreeSpirit. I adore the diversity of the jewel tones Anna Maria used; the fabrics speak for themselves in this quilt. Thanks, Anna Maria!

Materials

Yardage is based on 42"-wide fabric, unless otherwise noted.

4½ yards of light-yellow print for blocks, sashing, and inner border

1⅛ yards of blue-and-green print for blocks

1 yard of blue-and-purple print for blocks and outer border

¾ yard of green print for blocks

¾ yard of violet print for blocks

¾ yard of orange-and-blue print for outer border

⅜ yard *each* of pink print and dark-yellow print for blocks

⅜ yard of purple print for blocks

1 fat quarter *each* of light-blue print and navy-and-green print for blocks

⅔ yard of fabric for binding

7½ yards of orange print for backing

86" x 102" piece of batting

Cutting

From the *lengthwise grain* of the light-yellow print, cut:
16 strips, 2½" x 80½"; cut *4 of the strips* into:
2 strips, 2½" x 68½"
64 squares, 2½" x 2½" (B)

From the *crosswise grain* of the remaining light-yellow print, cut:
27 strips, 2½" x 42"; crosscut into:
388 squares, 2½" x 2½" (B)
20 rectangles, 2½" x 4½" (L)

From the green print, cut:
5 strips, 4½" x 42"; crosscut into 36 squares, 4½" x 4½" (A)

From the purple print, cut:
5 strips, 4½" x 42"; crosscut into 36 squares, 4½" x 4½" (A)

From the blue-and-green print, cut:
8 strips, 4½" x 42"; crosscut into:
4 rectangles, 4½" x 28½" (C)
4 rectangles, 4½" x 8½" (D)
4 rectangles, 4½" x 22½" (E)
4 rectangles, 4½" x 14½" (F)

From the violet print, cut:
2 strips, 4½" x 42"; crosscut into:
2 rectangles, 4½" x 12½" (G)
1 rectangle, 4½" x 10½" (H)
2 rectangles, 4½" x 8½" (I)

From the pink print, cut:
2 strip, 4½" x 42"; crosscut into:
1 rectangle, 4½" x 14½" (J)
3 rectangles, 4½" x 10½" (H)

From the dark-yellow print, cut:
  2 strips, 4½" x 42"; crosscut into:
    2 rectangles, 4½" x 14½" (J)
    1 rectangle, 4½" x 10½" (H)
    1 rectangle, 4½" x 8½" (I)

From the blue-and-purple print, cut:
  7 strips, 4½" x 42"; crosscut *2 of the strips* into:
    1 rectangle, 4½" x 14½" (J)
    2 rectangles, 4½" x 12½" (G)
    1 rectangle, 4½" x 8½" (I)

From the light-blue print, cut:
  4 strips, 4½" x 18"; crosscut into:
    2 rectangles, 4½" x 8½" (I)
    2 rectangles, 4½" x 10½" (H)

From the navy-and-green print, cut:
  4 strips, 4½" x 18" crosscut into:
    1 rectangle, 4½" x 16½" (K)
    1 rectangle, 4½" x 10½" (H)
    2 rectangles, 4½" x 8½" (I)

From the orange-and-blue print, cut:
  5 strips, 4½" x 42"

From the orange print, cut:
  9 strips, 2¼" x 42"

Assembling the Blocks

1. Draw a diagonal line from corner to corner on the wrong side of each light-yellow B square. Place marked squares on diagonally opposite corners of a green A square. Sew along the marked line. Trim away the corner fabric, leaving a ¼" seam allowance. Press the seam allowances toward the resulting light-yellow triangle. Place marked squares on the two remaining corners of the green A square. Sew, trim, and press to make one unit. Make a total of 36 units.

Make 36.

2. Repeat step 1 using the purple A squares and 144 of the marked light-yellow B squares to make 36 units.

Make 36.

3. Repeating step 1, sew four marked light-yellow B squares to each blue-and-green C, D, E, and F rectangle to make four of each unit.

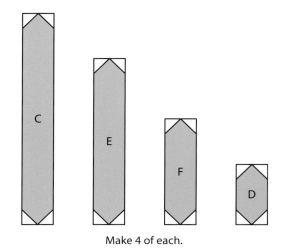

Make 4 of each.

4. In the same way, sew four marked light-yellow B squares to *each* of the following rectangles:
   • Violet G, H, and I rectangles
   • Pink H and J rectangles
   • Dark-yellow H, I, and J rectangles
   • Blue-and-purple G, I, and J rectangles
   • Light-blue H and I rectangles
   • Navy-and-green H, I, and K rectangles

Assembling the Quilt Top

1. Lay out the units and light-yellow L rectangles in 11 vertical rows as shown in the quilt assembly diagram on page 49. Join the pieces into rows. The rows should measure 80½" long. Press the seam allowances in one direction.

2. Sew the rows and 10 of the light-yellow 80½"-long strips together to complete the quilt top center. Press the seam allowances toward the light-yellow rows. The quilt center should measure 64½" x 80½".

3. Sew the 80½"-long strips to opposite sides of the quilt center. Press the seam allowances toward the light-yellow strips. Sew the 68½"-long strips to the top and bottom of the quilt top to complete the inner border.

4. Join the remaining blue-and-purple strips end to end. From the pieced strip, cut one 84½"-long strip and one 76½"-long strip.

5. Join the orange-and-blue strips end to end. From the pieced strip, cut one 84½"-long strip and one 76½"-long strip.

6. Sew the blue-and-purple 84½"-long strip to the right side of the quilt top. Sew the orange-and-blue 84½"-long strip to the left side of the quilt top. Press the seam allowances toward the just-added strips.

7. Sew the blue-and-purple 76½"-long strip to the bottom of the quilt top. Sew the orange-and-blue 76½"-long strip to the top of the quilt top to complete the outer border. Press the seam allowances toward the just-added strips.

Finishing

1. Cut the backing fabric into three equal lengths and remove the selvage edges. Sew the lengths together and trim the sides to make an 86" x 102" backing.

2. Layer and baste the backing, batting, and quilt top. Quilt as desired.

3. Referring to "Binding Your Quilt" (page 76) and using the orange 2¼"-wide strips, make and attach binding. Make a label with your name, date, and thoughtful message to the receiver; sew to the back of the quilt to finish.

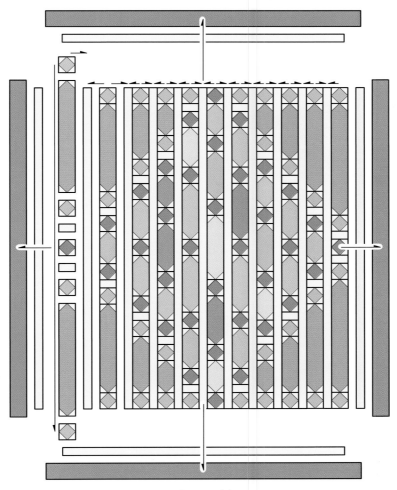

Quilt assembly

Drawers

W atching the movers load the truck for one of our moves, I was inspired to sketch a chest of drawers. That sketch developed into this design. I took my color cues from a contemporary mural on the side of a building. Inspiration can come from anywhere!

"Drawers," pieced by Susan Guzman and Linda Barrett and machine quilted by Linda Barrett	Finished quilt: 80½" x 84½" Finished blocks: 6" x 10", 8" x 10", and 10" x 10"

The FABRICS

I ended up making a few extra blocks in my favorite colors and swapped them out with less vibrant colors to liven things up! Purchase a bit more of your favorites to do the same. For this quilt, I used the Bella Solids collection by Moda.

Materials

Yardage is based on 42"-wide fabric, unless otherwise noted.

⅝ yard *each* of 16 assorted green, pink, brown, red, orange, purple, and blue solids for blocks

1⅔ yards of ivory solid for blocks

⅔ yard of lime-green solid for binding

8 yards of fabric for backing

90" x 94" piece of batting

Cutting

From *each* of the 16 solids, cut:
    4 strips, 2½" x 42"; crosscut into:
        7 squares, 2½" x 2½" (112 total; A)
        3 rectangles, 2½" x 4½" (48 total; B)
        10 rectangles, 2½" x 10½" (160 total; C)
    1 strip, 6½" x 42"; crosscut into:
        3 rectangles, 2½" x 6½" (48 total; D)
        2 rectangles, 4½" x 6½" (32 total; E)

From the ivory solid, cut:
    21 strips, 2½" x 42"; crosscut into:
        112 squares, 2½" x 2½" (F)
        64 rectangles, 2½" x 4½" (G)
        32 rectangles, 2½" x 6½" (H)

From the lime-green solid, cut:
    9 strips, 2¼" x 42"

Assembling the Quilt Top

1. Join three ivory F squares and two matching solid A squares to make a pieced strip. Press the seam allowances toward the A squares.

2. Sew C rectangles that match the A squares, to opposite sides of the pieced strip from step 1 to complete block 1. Press the seam allowances toward the C rectangles. Make a total of 16 blocks.

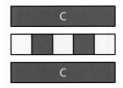 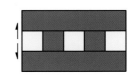

Block 1
Make 16.

3. Join three matching assorted solid B rectangles and two ivory G rectangles to make a rectangular unit. Press the seam allowances toward the B rectangles.

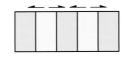

4. Sew C rectangles that match the B rectangles, to opposite sides of the rectangular unit from step 3 to complete block 2. Press the seam allowances toward the C rectangles. Make a total of 16 blocks.

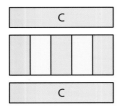
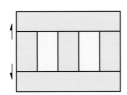

Block 2
Make 16.

5. Join three matching solid A squares and two ivory F squares to make a pieced strip. Press the seam allowances toward the A squares.

6. Sew C rectangles that match the A squares, to opposite sides of the pieced strip from step 5 to complete block 3. Press the seam allowances toward the C rectangles. Make a total of 16 blocks.

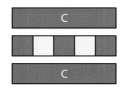
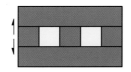

Block 3
Make 16.

7. Join three matching solid D rectangles and two ivory H rectangles to make a rectangular unit. Press the seam allowances toward the D rectangles.

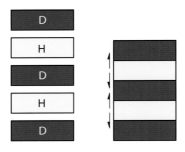

8. Sew C rectangles that match the D rectangles to opposite sides of the rectangular unit from step 8 to complete block 4. Press the seam allowances toward the C rectangles. Make a total of 16 blocks.

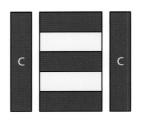

Block 4
Make 16.

9. Join two ivory F squares and one solid A square to make a pieced strip. Press the seam allowances toward the A square.

10. Sew E rectangles that match the A square to opposite sides of the pieced strip from step 9 to complete block 5. Press the seam allowances toward the E rectangles. Make a total of 16 blocks.

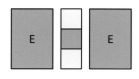

Block 5
Make 16.

11. Join two ivory G rectangles and one solid A square to make a pieced strip. Press the seam allowances toward the A square.

 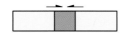

12. Sew C rectangles that match the A square to opposite sides of the pieced strip from step 11 to complete block 6. Press the seam allowances toward the C rectangles. Make a total of 16 blocks.

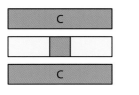 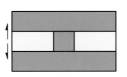

Block 6
Make 16.

Assembling the Quilt Top

1. Lay out blocks in eight vertical rows of 12 blocks each as shown in the quilt assembly diagram below. Each row contains block 1–6, repeated twice, and even rows are rotated 180° so that block 6 is at the top. Join the blocks into rows. Press the seam allowances in opposite directions from row to row.

2. Join the rows and press the seam allowances in one direction.

Quilt assembly

Finishing

1. Cut the backing fabric into three equal lengths and remove the selvage edges. Sew the lengths together and trim the sides to make a 90" x 94" backing.

2. Layer and baste the backing, batting, and quilt top. Quilt as desired.

3. Referring to "Binding Your Quilt" (page 76) and using the lime-green 2¼"-wide strips, make and attach binding. Make a label with your name, date, and thoughtful message to the receiver; sew to the back of the quilt to finish.

Candy Bar Lane

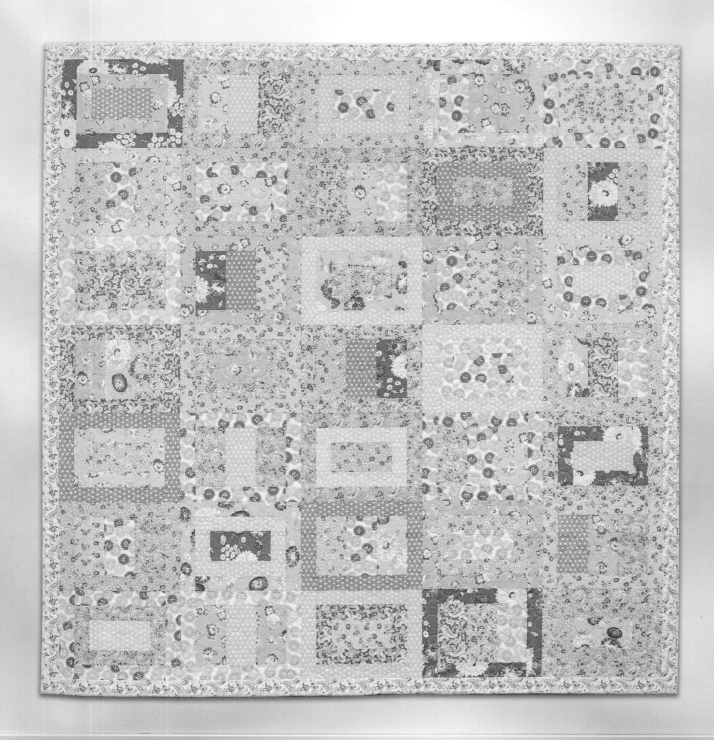

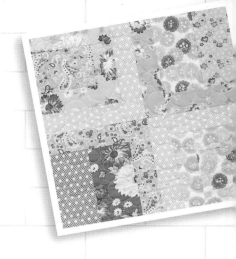

*T*his design is a variation of my most popular pattern, "Candy Bar Road." The center rectangles of both blocks remind me of large chocolate bars. Treat yourself to your favorite candy bar and start making this fast bed-sized quilt.

"Candy Bar Lane," pieced by Susan Guzman and machine quilted by Linda Barrett

Finished quilt: 84½" x 88½"
Finished blocks: 12" x 16"

The FABRICS

For this quilt, I used fabrics from the Scrumptious collection by Bonnie and Camille for Moda. After laying out my patches, I decided to replace a few with two additional fabrics. If you wish to do the same, purchase a few extra fat quarters.

Materials

Yardage is based on 42"-wide fabric, unless otherwise noted.

½ yard *each* of 17 assorted red, green, orange, turquoise, and pink prints for blocks

1 fat quarter of coordinating print for blocks

1⅜ yards of white print for borders and binding

8¼ yards for backing

94" x 98" piece of batting

Cutting

From *each* ½ yard of assorted prints, cut:
  1 strip, 4½" x 42"; crosscut into 4 rectangles,
    4½" x 8½" (68 total; A)
  4 strips, 2½" x 42"; crosscut into:
    4 rectangles, 2½" x 8½" (68 total; B)
    8 rectangles, 2½" x 12½" (136 total; C)

From the coordinating fat quarter, cut:
  4 strips, 2½" x 21"; crosscut into:
    4 rectangles, 2½" x 12½" (C)
    4 rectangles, 2½" x 8½" (B)
  1 strip, 4½" x 21"; crosscut into 1 rectangle,
    4½" x 8½" (A)

From the white print, cut:
  9 strips, 2½" x 42"
  9 strips, 2¼" x 42"

Assembling Block 1

For each block, you'll need three different prints in the following combination: one A rectangle, four matching B rectangles, and four matching C rectangles. Directions are for making one block.

1. Sew print B rectangles to both long edges of a print A rectangle. Press the seam allowances toward the B rectangles. Sew print B rectangles to the ends of the unit to make a center unit. Press the seam allowances toward the B rectangles.

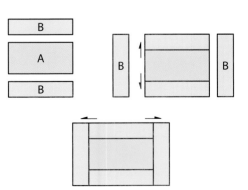

> *Plan to cut a few extra pieces so that you'll still have plenty of options for mixing and matching when you get to the final block.*

2. Sew print C rectangles to both long edges of the center unit. Press the seam allowances toward the C rectangles. Sew print C rectangles to the ends of the unit to complete block 1. Press the seam allowances toward the C rectangles.

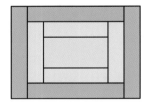

3. Repeat steps 1 and 2 to make a total of 18 blocks.

Block 1
Make 18.

Assembling Block 2

For each block, you'll need three assorted A rectangles and four matching C rectangles. Directions are for making one block.

1. Sew three print A rectangles together as shown to make a rectangular unit. Press the seam allowances in one direction.

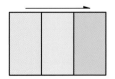

2. Sew print C rectangles to both long edges of the center unit. Press the seam allowances toward the C rectangles. Sew print C rectangles to the ends of the unit to complete block 2. Press the seam allowances toward the center unit.

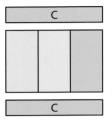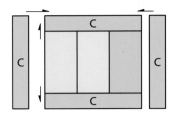

3. Repeat steps 1 and 2 to make a total of 17 blocks.

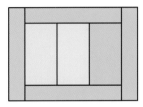

Block 2
Make 17.

Tip | Add More Contrast

The fabric collection chosen for this design is feminine and pretty, offering a subtle visual effect. For a higher impact, consider adding more contrast by choosing an equal combination of light, medium, and dark fabrics.

Assembling the Quilt Top

1. Lay out the blocks in seven rows of five blocks each, alternating blocks 1 and 2 in each row as shown in the quilt assembly diagram on page 57. Sew the blocks together into rows. Press the seam allowances in opposite directions from row to row. Sew the rows together and press the seam allowances in one direction. The quilt center should measure 80½" x 84½".

2. Sew the white strips together end to end. From the pieced strip, cut four 84½"-long strips. Sew white strips to opposite sides of quilt center. Press the seam allowances toward the white strips. Sew white strips to the top and bottom of the quilt top to complete the border. Press the seam allowances toward the white strips.

Finishing

1. Cut the backing fabric into three equal lengths and remove the selvage edges. Sew the lengths together and trim the sides to make a 94" x 98" backing.

2. Layer and baste the backing, batting, and quilt top. Quilt as desired.

3. Referring to "Binding Your Quilt" (page 76) and using the white 2¼"-wide strips, make and attach binding. Make a label with your name, date, and thoughtful message to the receiver; sew to the back of the quilt to finish.

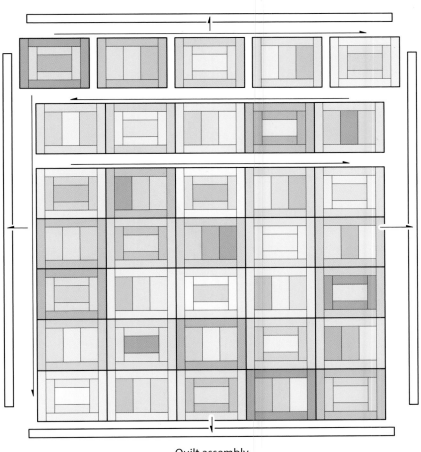

Quilt assembly

Kindred Spirit

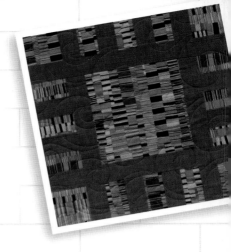

A kindred spirit is someone with whom we feel a special connection. It might be someone we know personally or someone we admire from afar. I feel this connection with certain fabric designers. There's a kinship I feel toward their artistry; their gorgeous fabrics bring me great joy!

"Kindred Spirit," pieced by Susan Guzman and machine quilted by Linda Barrett

Finished quilt: 96½" x 96½"
Finished blocks: 22" x 22"

The FABRICS

I've long been drawn to the fabrics designed by Kaffe Fassett and his amazing team that includes Phillip Jacobs and Brandon Mably. In this quilt, two slightly different colored shot cottons form the sashing in the blocks. To bring uniformity into the design, I used only one of them for the pieced border.

Materials

Yardage is based on 42"-wide fabric, unless otherwise noted.

½ yard *each* of 16 large-scale blue, red, yellow, orange, brown, green, and black prints for blocks and border

3¼ yards of plum shot cotton for blocks, border, and binding*

2⅞ yards of dark-blue shot cotton for blocks*

9¼ yards of fabric for backing

106" x 106" piece of batting

A shot cotton uses one thread color for the warp and a different thread color for the weft, giving the fabric depth and visual interest. If you prefer, you can substitute a solid fabric.

Cutting

From *each of 12* large-scale prints, cut:
1 strip, 10½" x 42"; crosscut into:
    1 square, 10½" x 10½" (12 total; A)
    6 squares, 4½" x 4½" (72 total; B)
1 strip, 4½" x 42"; crosscut into 15 rectangles, 2½" x 4½" (180 total; C)

From *each of 4* large-scale prints, cut:
1 strip, 10½" x 42"; crosscut into:
    1 square, 10½" x 10½" (4 total; A)
    7 squares, 4½" x 4½" (28 total; B)
1 strip, 4½" x 42"; crosscut into 15 rectangles, 2½" x 4½" (60 total; C)

From the dark-blue shot cotton, cut:
18 strips, 2½" x 42"; crosscut into:
    108 rectangles, 2½" x 4½" (D)
    18 rectangles, 2½" x 10½" (E)
2 strips, 22½" x 42"; crosscut into 18 rectangles, 2½" x 22½" (F)

From the plum shot cotton, cut:
1 strip, 22½" x 42"; crosscut into 14 rectangles, 2½" x 22½" (F)
1 strip, 10½" x 42"; crosscut into 14 rectangles, 2½" x 10½" (E)
19 strips, 2½" x 42"; crosscut into 148 rectangles, 2½" x 4½" (D)
10 strips, 2¼" x 42"

Tip | Plan Ahead

You'll have enough to make nine blocks using the blue shot cotton and seven blocks using the plum. I purposely mixed up their placement in the design. Follow what I did, or come up with your own configuration. Either way, it's a good thing to plan where you'd like to see your prized prints and what sashing color you'd like to use. Have fun!

Assembling the Blocks

For each block, you'll need one A square, four B squares, and 12 C rectangles from one large-scale print. You'll also need 12 D rectangles, two E rectangles, and two F rectangles from one shot cotton. Lay out the pieces for each block as shown in the block assembly diagrams and make any adjustments before you begin sewing. Directions are for making one block.

1. Sew three print C rectangles and two shot-cotton D rectangles together to make a rectangular unit. Press the seam allowances toward the D rectangles. Sew a shot-cotton E rectangle to the right side of the unit to make a side unit. Repeat to make a second unit.

Make 2.

If you've never used shot cottons, seek them out and give them a try. They add a bit more spark then a plain solid.

2. Sew the side units from step 1 to opposite sides of a print A square. Press the seam allowances toward the side units. Sew shot-cotton F rectangles to the top and bottom of the unit to complete the block center. Press the seam allowances toward the F rectangles.

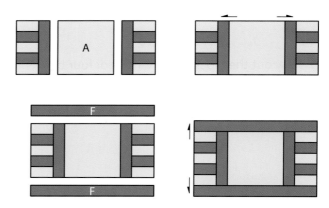

3. Sew together two print B squares, four shot-cotton D rectangles, and three print C rectangles to make a pieced strip. Press the seam allowances toward the D rectangles. Repeat to make a second unit.

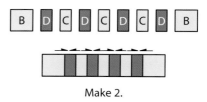

Make 2.

4. Sew a pieced strip from step 3 to the top and bottom of the block center to complete the block. Press the seam allowances toward the block center.

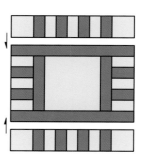

5. Repeat the steps to make a total of 16 blocks, nine with blue shot cotton and seven with plum shot cotton.

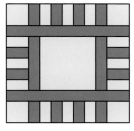
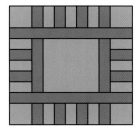

Make 9.   Make 7.

Assembling the Quilt Top

1. Lay out the blocks in four rows of four blocks each as shown in the quilt assembly diagram, right. Sew the blocks together into rows. Press the seam allowances in opposite directions from row to row. Join the rows to complete the quilt center. Press the seam allowances in one direction.

2. Using B squares and C rectangles from one large-scale print, sew together two B squares, three C rectangles, and four plum D rectangles to make a border unit as shown. Press the seam allowances toward the large-scale print pieces. Make a total of 16 units.

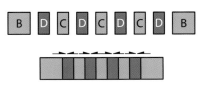

Make 16.

3. Join four border units end to end to make a side border. Press the seam allowances in one direction. Repeat to make a second side border. Sew the borders to opposite sides of the quilt center. Press the seam allowance toward the center.

4. Join four borders units end to end to make a top border strip. Press the seam allowances in one direction. Sew a print B square to each end of the border strip. Press the seam allowances toward the B squares. Repeat to make a bottom border. Sew these borders to the top and bottom of the quilt. Press the seam allowances toward the just-added strips.

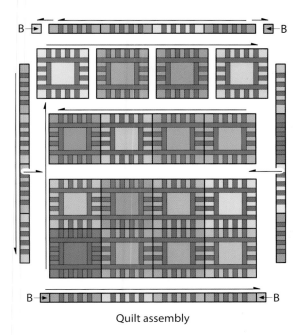

Quilt assembly

Finishing

1. Cut the backing fabric into three equal lengths and remove the selvage edges. Sew the lengths together and trim the sides to make a 106" x 106" backing.

2. Layer and baste the backing, batting, and quilt top. Quilt as desired.

3. Referring to "Binding Your Quilt" (page 76) and using the plum 2¼"-wide strips, make and attach binding. Make a label with your name, date, and thoughtful message to the receiver; sew to the back of the quilt to finish.

Garden Mews

I've always thought it would be cool to own a former carriage house, with living quarters above and a stable below. Mine would be in the city, and there'd be a cozy, secret garden in the back surrounded by a stone wall—as the dark-gray solid in this quilt encloses the floral prints.

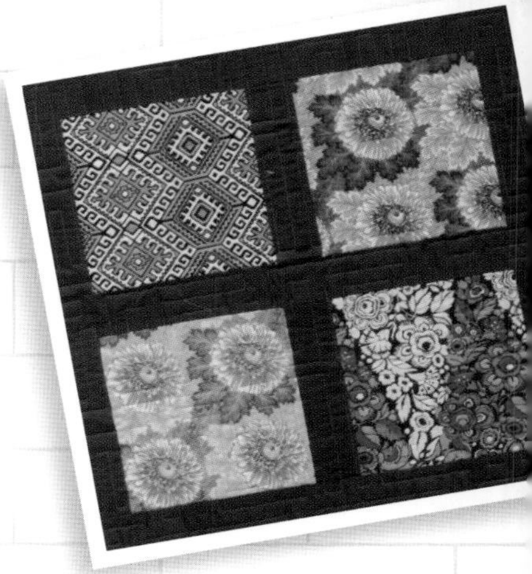

"Garden Mews," pieced and machine quilted by Linda Barrett

Finished quilt: 106½" x 106½"

The FABRICS

The unusual combination of florals and geometric shapes in Amy Butler's Hapi collection for Rowan lends interest to the structured, clean-line design. Consider using a voile print from the same collection to back your quilt, as I did.

Materials

Yardage is based on 42"-wide fabric, unless otherwise noted.

⅝ yard *each* of 11 assorted large-scale blue, gray, black, red, pink, ivory, green, orange, and purple prints for squares

6½ yards of dark-gray solid for sashing, borders, and binding

1⅞ yards of ivory solid for sashing and borders

⅜ yard of coordinating large-scale print for squares

10 yards of fabric for backing

116" x 116" piece of batting

Cutting

From the *lengthwise grain* of the dark-gray solid, cut:

- 15 strips, 2½" x 102½" (B)
- 13 strips, 2½" x 106½"; crosscut *11 of the strips* into:
  - 78 squares, 2½" x 2½" (D)
  - 104 rectangles, 2½" x 8½" (E)

From the *crosswise grain* of the dark-gray solid, cut:

- 10 strips, 2¼" x 42"

From the ivory solid, cut:

- 3 strips, 2½" x 42"; crosscut into 36 squares, 2½" x 2½" (F)
- 6 strips, 8½" x 42"; crosscut into 96 rectangles, 2½" x 8½" (G)

From *each of 3* large-scale prints, cut:

- 2 strips, 8½" x 42"; crosscut into 7 squares, 8½" x 8½" (21 total; A)

From *each of 8* large-scale prints, cut:

- 2 strips, 8½" x 42"; crosscut into 5 squares, 8½" x 8½" (40 total; A)

From the coordinating large-scale print, cut:

- 1 strip, 8½" x 42"; crosscut into 3 squares, 8½" x 8½" (A)

Assembling the Quilt Top

1. Sew six ivory F squares, eight ivory G rectangles, and 13 dark-gray D squares together as shown to make a pieced sashing strip as shown, right. Press the seam allowances toward the D squares. Make a total of six strips.

2. On a design wall or other flat area, lay out the ivory G rectangles, dark-gray E rectangles, and print A squares in eight rows. Each row will have six G rectangles, 13 E rectangles, and eight A squares. Rearrange the A squares until you are pleased with the arrangement, referring to "Tips for Coloring a Design" (page 9) as needed. Join the pieces into rows as shown, far right. Press the seam allowances toward the E rectangles.

3. Return the rows from step 2 to your design wall. Place the pieced sashing rows from step 1 and the dark-gray B strips between the rows as shown in the quilt assembly diagram on page 65. Join the rows and dark-gray strips to complete the quilt center. Press the seam allowances toward the dark-gray strips. The quilt center should measure 102½" x 102½".

Tip | Aligning the Rows

When joining the pieced rows and dark-gray strips, it's important for the seam lines of the pieced rows to line up on each side of the dark-gray strips. One easy way to make sure the seams line up is to mark the gray strip with pins to show where the seams need to match. Then join the rows and dark-gray strips, matching the seam line with the pins.

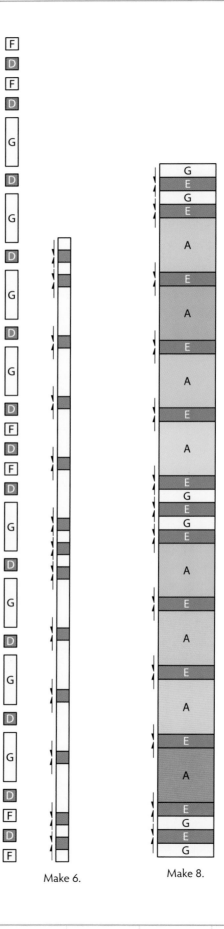

Make 6.

Make 8.

> *This quilt design started with the distinctive border, which is based on a watchband I spied in a catalog.*

4. Sew the remaining dark-gray 102½"-long strips to opposite sides of the quilt center. Press the seam allowances toward the dark-gray strips. Sew the dark-gray 106½"-long strips to the top and bottom of the quilt to complete the border. Press the seam allowances toward the dark-gray strips.

Finishing

1. Cut the backing fabric into three equal lengths and remove the selvage edges. Sew the lengths together and trim the sides to make a 116" x 116" backing.

2. Layer and baste the backing, batting, and quilt top. Quilt as desired.

3. Referring to "Binding Your Quilt" (page 76) and using the dark-gray 2¼"-wide strips, make and attach binding. Make a label with your name, date, and thoughtful message to the receiver; sew to the back of the quilt to finish.

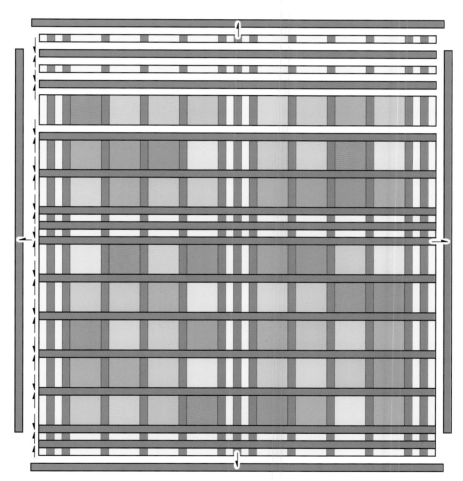

Quilt assembly

*S*an Francisco is one of the most exciting cities in the United States, with so much to enjoy: sightseeing, marvelous art galleries, delicious cuisine, historical sites. The sharp elbow turns in this quilt remind me of the city's famous Lombard Street.

"Summertime on Lombard Street," pieced by Susan Guzman and machine quilted by Linda Barrett

Finished quilt: 110½" x 100½"
Finished blocks: 5" x 10" and 5" x 5"

The FABRICS

Art Gallery Fabrics create a warm, summery king-size quilt. To make a queen-size quilt, eliminate four vertical rows from the quilt center; see "Making a Different-Sized Quilt" (page 75). Use the extra blocks and fabric to make a throw or baby quilt.

Materials

Yardage is based on 42"-wide fabric, unless otherwise noted.

¾ yard *each* of 18 assorted yellow, blue, green, and pink prints for blocks and outer border

8¼ yards of ivory solid for blocks

1⅞ yards of green print for inner border

⅞ yard of blue print for binding

9⅝ yards for backing

110" x 120" piece of batting

Cutting

From *each of 8* assorted prints, cut:
  4 strips, 5½" x 42"; crosscut into:
    8 rectangles, 5½" x 10½" (64 total; A)
    10 squares, 5½" x 5½" (80 total; E)

From *each of 10* assorted prints, cut:
  2 strips, 10½" x 42"; crosscut into 8 rectangles, 5½" x 10½" (80 total; A)

From the ivory solid, cut:
  42 strips, 5½" x 42"; crosscut into 288 squares, 5½" x 5½" (B)
  12 strips, 3" x 42"; crosscut into 144 squares, 3" x 3" (C)

From the green print, cut:
  11 strips, 5½" x 42"; crosscut into 72 squares, 5½" x 5½" (D)

From the blue print, cut:
  11 strips, 2¼" x 42"

Assembling the Blocks

1. Draw a diagonal line from corner to corner on the wrong side of each ivory B square. Place a marked square on one corner of a print A rectangle. Sew along the marked line. Trim away the corner fabric, leaving a ¼" seam allowance. Press the seam allowances toward the resulting ivory triangle. Make a total of 72 units.

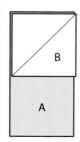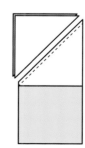

> *A pop of color for the inner border adds an unexpected element.*

2. Sew a marked B square on the opposite end of each unit from step 1, making sure to orient the square as shown to complete the block. The block should measure 5½" x 10½". Press the seam allowances toward the resulting ivory triangle. Make a total of 72 units.

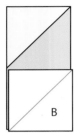 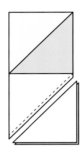 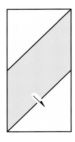

Make 72.

3. Repeat steps 1 and 2 using the remaining marked B squares and print A rectangles to make 72 blocks, making sure to reverse the orientation of the B squares as shown.

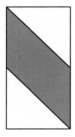

Make 72.

Assembling the Quilt Top

1. Lay out the blocks in eight rows of 18 blocks each, making sure to orient the blocks as shown in the quilt assembly diagram on page 69. Sew the blocks into rows. Press the seam allowances in opposite directions from row to row. Join the rows to complete the quilt center. Press the seam allowances in one direction.

2. To make the border blocks, draw a diagonal line from corner to corner on the wrong side of each ivory C square. Place marked squares on diagonally opposite corners of a green D square. Sew along the marked line. Trim away the corner fabric, leaving a ¼" seam allowance. Press the seam allowances toward the resulting ivory triangles. Make a total of 72 border blocks.

Make 72.

| Tip | Directional Prints |

If you're using a directional print for the D squares, place marked ivory C squares on the top-left and bottom-right corners of 36 squares. Place marked squares on the top-right and bottom-left corners of the remaining 36 squares.

3. For the inner border, join 16 border blocks, rotating every other block as shown to make a side border strip. Press the seam allowances in one direction. Repeat to make a second side border strip. In the same way, join 20 border blocks to make a top border. Press the seam allowances in the directions indicated. Repeat to make a bottom border strip.

Side borders
Make 2.

Top and bottom borders
Make 2.

4. Sew the inner-border strips to the sides, top, and bottom of the quilt center, making sure to rotate the border strips as shown in the quilt assembly diagram.

5. For the outer border, randomly join 18 E squares to make a side border strip. Press the seam allowances in one direction. Repeat to make a second side border strip. Randomly join 22 print E squares to make a top border. Press the seam allowances in one direction. Repeat to make a bottom border strip.

6. Sew the outer border strips to the sides, top, and bottom of the quilt top as shown in the quilt assembly diagram.

Finishing

1. Cut the backing fabric into three equal lengths and remove the selvage edges. Sew the lengths together and trim the sides to make a 110" x 120" backing.

2. Layer and baste the backing, batting, and quilt top. Quilt as desired.

3. Referring to "Binding Your Quilt" (page 76) and using the blue 2¼"-wide strips, make and attach binding. Make a label with your name, date, and thoughtful message to the receiver; sew to the back of the quilt to finish.

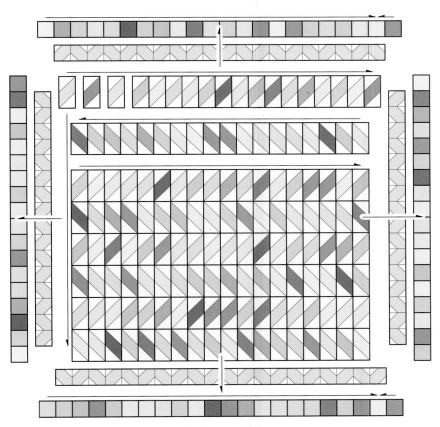

Quilt assembly

Good Fortune

My wish is that we all experience good fortune, but life often gives us challenges to overcome. I think of it as climbing a ladder, working through challenges and never giving up. I hope this quilt inspires you to do the same.

"Good Fortune," pieced by Susan Guzman and machine quilted by Linda Barrett

Finished quilt: 80½" x 80½"
Finished blocks: 20" x 20"

Materials

Yardage is based on 42"-wide fabric, unless otherwise noted.

16 fat quarters of assorted large-scale blue, pink, yellow, brown, orange, and green prints for blocks

1¼ yards *each* of 4 coordinating green, brown, navy, and yellow prints for blocks

⅔ yard of blue print for binding

7⅞ yards of fabric for backing

90" x 90" piece of batting

Cutting

From *each* assorted fat quarter, cut:
   2 strips, 2½" x 21"; crosscut into 2 rectangles, 2½" x 16½" (32 total; A)
   1 strip, 8½" x 21"; crosscut into 3 rectangles, 4½" x 8½" (48 total; B)

From *each* of the coordinating prints, cut:
   14 strips, 2½" x 42"; crosscut into:
      16 rectangles, 2½" x 16½" (64 total; A)
      8 rectangles, 2½" x 20½" (32 total; D)
      8 rectangles, 2½" x 8½" (32 total; C)

From the blue print, cut:
   9 strips, 2¼" x 42"

Assembling the Blocks

For each block, you'll need two A rectangles and three B rectangles from one large-scale print. You'll also need four A rectangles, two C rectangles, and two D rectangles from one coordinating print. Directions are for making one block.

1. Sew together two coordinating C rectangles and three large-scale B rectangles to make a center unit. Press the seam allowances toward the C rectangles.

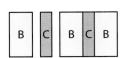 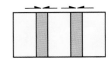

> *Rotating every other block means there are no seams to align except at block corners.*

2. Join one large-scale A rectangle and one coordinating A rectangle. Press the seam allowances toward the coordinating rectangle. Make two of these units and sew them to the top and bottom of the center unit. Press the seam allowances away from the center unit.

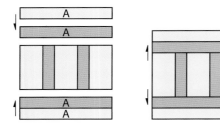

3. Sew coordinating A rectangles to opposite sides of the unit from step 2. Press the seam allowances toward the A rectangles. Sew coordinating D rectangles to the top and bottom of the unit to make one block. Press the seam allowances toward the D rectangles. Repeat the process to make a total of 16 blocks.

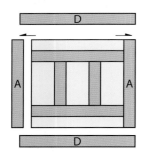 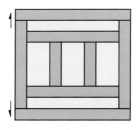

Make 16.

Tip | Add a POW factor!

This quilt has a lot of potential for adjusting to your personal taste. For the block sashing, I used prints that were the same design but four different colors. When choosing your fat quarters, consider more high-contrast fabrics to give this design more POW!

Assembling the Quilt Top

1. Lay out the blocks in four rows of four blocks each, rotating every other block as shown in the quilt assembly diagram below. Join the blocks into rows. Press the seam allowances in opposite directions from row to row.

2. Join the rows and press the seam allowances in one direction.

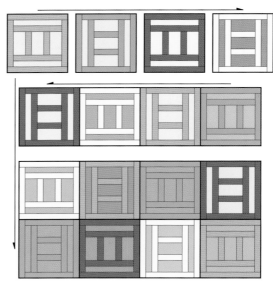

Quilt assembly

Finishing

1. Cut the backing fabric into three equal lengths and remove the selvage edges. Sew the lengths together and trim the sides to make a 90" x 90" backing.

2. Layer and baste the backing, batting, and quilt top. Quilt as desired.

3. Referring to "Binding Your Quilt" (page 76) and using the blue 2¼"-wide strips, make and attach binding. Make a label with your name, date, and thoughtful message to the receiver; sew to the back of the quilt to finish.

I have a few basic tips to share with you about certain supplies and techniques I like to use. For more details on any of the following techniques, go to ShopMartingale.com/HowtoQuilt for free downloadable information.

Basic Tools and Supplies

Personally, I don't use many quilters' gadgets. However, new tools are constantly being introduced to the marketplace to help make your quilting experience easier and fun, so I encourage you to try them if they appeal to you.

Here are the basic tools I use on a regular basis:

- 45 mm rotary cutter
- 24" x 36" cutting mat
- 6" x 24" acrylic ruler
- Extra-fine pins for piecing block patches
- Fine pins for heavier parts of the project, such as when pinning borders onto the sides of a large quilt top
- Scissors in two sizes: regular for cutting fabric and small for snipping threads

In addition, there are two supplies other than fabric that we all use—thread and batting.

Thread. Many thread companies produce quality threads. Whether sewing on my machine or working by hand, I prefer Aurifil thread because of its strength, the gorgeous range of colors, and especially how the 50-weight cotton virtually disappears into the fabric.

Batting. I've always been a cotton girl, whether it's shopping for clothing, linens, fabrics, or batting. Imagine my surprise when I realized how much more sense it makes for me to use 80% cotton/20% polyester batting; folding doesn't crease as harshly as with 100% cotton batting. I prefer Air-Lite brand for its quality.

Laundering Fabrics

It's always best to prewash your fabrics to allow for shrinkage to occur before your fabrics are cut. Most fabric companies today use colorfast dyes, but prewashing also removes any chance of bleeding. Additionally, this process washes out the sizing that's used in the printing process.

If you're concerned about bleeding, try one of the products on the market that eliminate bleeding, just to be safe.

Achieving the Perfect ¼" Seam

Every sewing machine has a unique way of stitching. I've found that you can sometimes receive different results whether you're sewing along the grain or on the bias. A combination of the two could throw you off in yet another direction, such as when you sew pieces together to make a block or sew blocks together to make your quilt top. In order to find out the best way to sew on your machine, I suggest you perform a test session.

Whenever I'm working on a new machine, I like to see where the fabric edge needs to hit on my presser foot or the sewing machine plate as I move it through the sewing process. For me, a scant ¼" seam allowance typically works best and seems to produce spot-on piecing. However, it's important to test your seam allowances for yourself, since every sewing machine behaves differently.

A helpful way to test your seam allowance is to cut three 2½" x 5" strips of fabric, and then sew them together along their long edges. Press the seam allowances to one side. The center strip should measure 2" wide. If not, adjust the seam allowance by taking a slightly wider or narrower seam allowance until you find the correct width.

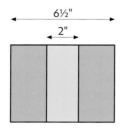

Trimming Selvage Edges

I'm sure you've noticed how selvage edges have holes in them along the length of the fabric. The holes happen during the printing process. You can certainly trim your edges to the holes and have access to a few extra microns of width to work with. However, keep in mind that most patterns are written with a cushion of a few inches and are based on 40"-wide fabric. With that said, I prefer to trim my selvages using the following method. For this example, I'll use a length of two yards.

1. Lay the two-yard length of fabric on your ironing board with the selvages to the right. You'll notice that the selvage edges typically do not line up straight from the bolt. With wrong sides together and securely holding the fold in your left hand, manipulate the edges with your right hand to line up the selvages. Press the fabric, including the fold, making adjustments to line up the edges as you press the length. Lay the pressed yardage on your cutting mat, placing the selvages to the right. Fold the length twice, aligning the selvages along a line on the mat.

2. Place your 6" x 24" ruler on top of your fabric. Align the ruler 1¼" from the outside selvage edges. Place your left hand on top of the ruler, and using a rotary cutter, cut off the selvages and save them in a large clear bag. Keep the bag handy to store more selvages later.

Cutting off selvages this way will allow you to have a generous amount of printed fabric still attached to the selvages to be used in selvage-friendly patterns or to use in an art quilt.

Borders

I'm a creature of habit when it comes to attaching borders to my quilt tops. I prefer to attach side borders first, and then I add top and bottom border strips. When using a print, I consider how I want that print to show when the quilt is on a bed. I don't like images to be upside-down, so I plan and cut my border strips accordingly. Another preference is to not piece border strips if I can help it (although it does happen, such as with "Bejeweled" on page 46). Of course, this is personal preference; I simply find it easier to cut my border strips from the lengthwise grain and I feel the borders look better as one length of fabric.

Pressing

When assembling your quilt blocks into rows, press the seam allowances in opposite directions from row to row. For example: rows 1, 3, and 5, press the seam allowances toward the right; rows 2 and 4, press toward the left. I prefer to use a dry iron with Mary Ellen's Best Press spray. I especially like the lavender scent because it's so clean and fresh.

When sewing rows together to finish your quilt top, I press the seam allowance in one direction. I've found it easiest to press the seam allowances away from me.

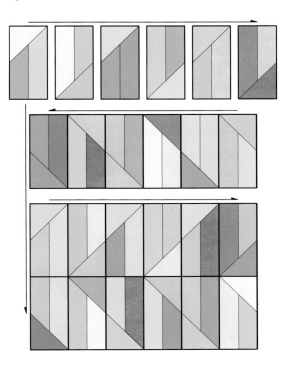

Making a Different-Sized Quilt

Typically, quilts are designed for a specific size. Some quilts can lose their appeal if they're resized, so you may want to take that into consideration. To keep the original design intact when converting a small quilt into something larger, you can always add borders to increase the size.

Decreasing the size of a quilt may be more challenging, depending on the design. However, "Summertime on Lombard Street" (page 66) can easily be made into a queen-size quilt by simply removing four vertical rows from the center and borders.

Remove 4 rows.

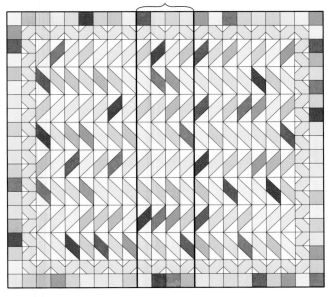

King size

Queen size

If you're unsure about how to change the size of a quilt, ask a trusted quilting friend, or visit your local quilt shop and ask if they can help you resize a pattern. This will help you avoid over- or under-buying what you'll need.

Basting a Quilt Sandwich

There are several ways to baste your quilt sandwich. When I'm quilting a quilt top on my machine, I'm usually on a tight deadline, so I rely quite heavily on spray basting my quilt sandwich before I begin quilting.

Other ways to baste include:

- **Using curved quilter's safety pins.** I space my safety pins by placing the length of my hand between pins.

- **Using needle and thread.** Make long stitches from side to side. I like to baste with needle and thread vertically and horizontally across the quilt sandwich. Basting this way will alleviate most of the shifting of the layers.

Binding Your Quilt

Read through the instructions first before making your binding. Although I prefer the look of hand-sewn binding, often I'm pressed for time, so I attach the binding to the **back** of my quilt and machine stitch it in place to the **front** of the quilt. Here are the steps for this faster way of attaching binding.

1. Cut the 2¼"-wide strips as directed in the project instructions. Join the strips end to end to make one long strip. Join strips at right angles with right sides together; stitch across the corner diagonally as shown using a ¼" seam allowance. Press the seam allowance open.

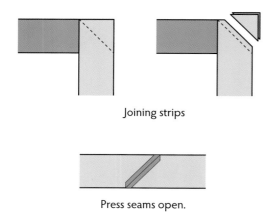

Joining strips

Press seams open.

2. Press the strip in half lengthwise, wrong sides together and raw edges aligned.

3. Starting in the middle of one side and aligning the raw edges, place an end of the binding strip on the back of the quilt. Begin stitching 8" to 10" from the start of the strip using a ¼" seam allowance. Stop stitching ¼" from a corner with a backstitch or two.

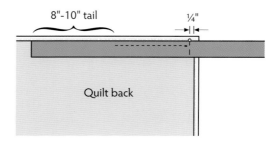

8"-10" tail

¼"

Quilt back

4. Turn the quilt 90° so that you'll be stitching along the next side. Fold the binding up away from the quilt; then fold it back down onto itself, even with the raw edge of the quilt top and finger-press the corner folds. Begin with a backstitch at the fold of the binding and continue stitching along the edge of the quilt top, mitering each corner as you come to it.

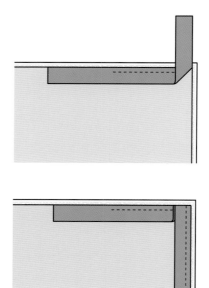

5. Stop stitching 8" to 10" from the starting point with a backstitch and remove the quilt from the machine. Lay the quilt edge on a flat surface. Fold the ending strip back as shown, mark the strip 2¼" from the fold, and cut off the excess strip.

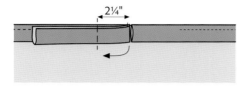

6. Gather the unsewn portion of the quilt edge into a pleat and pin in place. This will make it easier to sew the binding ends together. Unfold the binding strips and overlap the ends at right angles, right sides together as shown. Pin the ends together and draw a line diagonally from corner to corner.

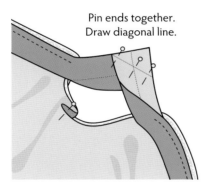

Pin ends together.
Draw diagonal line.

7. Sew along the drawn line. Trim the excess fabric, leaving a ¼" seam allowance. Remove the pins. Press the seam allowances open, and then refold the binding strip and sew it in place on the quilt.

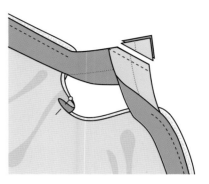

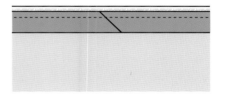

8. From the back of the quilt, press the binding away from the quilt. Fold the binding over the raw edges of the quilt sandwich to the front. Cover the row of machine stitching with the folded edge.

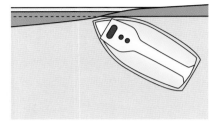

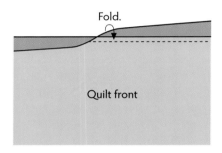

Fold.

Quilt front

9. Place the quilt edge under the presser foot, with the needle a few threads in from the edge of the binding. Starting with a backstitch and using a slightly longer stitch length (about 3 mm), slowly sew along the folded edge. Sewing more than a few threads from the folded edge can give you what I like to call a piecrust edge, where the edge curls up and looks like a piecrust. The result is a finished edge that looks a little less polished.

10. When you're about 5" from the first corner, fold a miter in the corner as shown and insert a pin. Continue sewing up to the corner, pull out the pin, and stop where the corner points overlap, making sure the needle is in the down position. Pivot the quilt 90° and continue sewing, mitering the corners as you go.

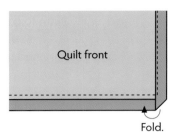

Quilt front

Fold.

11. When you reach the spot where you started, sew several stitches beyond the start point and backstitch.

I gratefully thank the following companies for providing quality products to construct the projects in this book:

Batting

Air-Lite Manufacturing
QuiltBattingPlus.com

Fabric

Alison Glass Design
AlisonGlass.com

Amy Butler Design
AmyButlerDesign.com

Anna Maria Horner
AnnaMariaHorner.com

Andover Fabrics
AndoverFabrics.com

Art Gallery Fabrics
ArtGalleryFabrics.com

BasicGrey
BasicGrey.com

Bonnie and Camille
CamilleRoskelley.typepad.com

Coats and Clark
CoatsandClark.com

FreeSpirit
WestminsterFabrics.com

Kaffe Fassett Studio
KaffeFassett.com

Lily Ashbury Design Studio
LilyAshbury.com

Michael Miller Fabrics
MichaelMillerFabrics.com

Moda
ModaFabrics.com

Parson Gray
ParsonGray.com

Pat Bravo Design
PatBravo.com

Rowan (Westminster Fabrics)
WestminsterFabrics.com

Tim Holtz
TimHoltz.com

Windham Fabrics
WindhamFabrics.net

Thread

Aurifil
Aurifil.com

Acknowledgments

My heartfelt thanks and gratitude to Lissa Alexander and Moda; Nancy Jewell and Westminster/Rowan/FreeSpirit/Coats and Clark; Alex Veronelli, Elena Grigotti, and Aurifil; Eric Herman and Air-Lite Manufacturing; Laura Jaquinto and Windham Fabrics; Pat Bravo Design and Art Gallery Fabrics; Alison Glass, Daryl Cohen, and Andover Fabrics; David and Amy Butler; Penny McMorris and Electric Quilt; and the entire team at Martingale, who were instrumental in helping me achieve the publishing of my first book. Your direction and guidance have helped me grow in so many ways. Thank you. Most importantly, I am deeply indebted to Beth Hayes, former editor in chief of *McCall's Quilting* magazine, for being a valued role model and friend. XOXO to all!

About the Author

With a background that includes trust banking and equity trading, interior design, architectural sales and marketing, and managing an art gallery, Susan Guzman's true passion is art and design. Susan fell in love with quilting when she joined an online quilt guild in 2004 and immediately participated in a variety of round robins to perfect her skills. Her eclectic background and creativity have helped her to develop a successful quilt-design business under the brand of SuzGuz Designs. Susan completed (with honors) the digital design program offered through The Art Institute of Pittsburgh's online division in January 2012. With these skills, she hopes to explore new aspects of design within the quilting and home-decor markets.

Since beginning her quilt-design business in 2006, Susan has written patterns and made quilts for more than 12 successful fabric companies and also created freelance projects for Amy Butler Design, FreeSpirit, Aurifil, Pfaff, and Husqvarna/Viking. Since 2008, she's had her designs published in *Asian Fabric, McCall's Quilting, McCall's Quick Quilts, Quilter's Home,* and *Quiltmaker's 100 Blocks* magazines. Check out Susan's website at www.SuzGuzDesigns.com.

About the Quilter

Linda Barrett of Threads and Traditions was born in Wales, United Kingdom. She began quilting by making a full-sized Celtic quilt in 1995. She brought the finished top with her when she moved to the United States in 2003, where she had it quilted by a professional long-arm quilter. Two years later, Linda bought her first long-arm machine and has been machine quilting ever since, adding a second system in 2007. She's the founding president of the Lexington (South Carolina) Quilt Guild and is an award-winning quilter. Twice Linda has had a quilt travel with the Hoffman Challenge, and since 2009, she's quilted masses of quilts designed by Susan Guzman for *McCall's Quilting* magazine.

Her first love will always be Celtic quilting. As with most quilters, Linda has more ideas than the time it would take to finish them! Visit her website at www.QuiltersExpress.com.